A Far From Home

Life in a Shelter
for Homeless Women

Lisa Ferrill

The Noble Press, Inc.

Printed in the United States of America

Library of Congress Cataloging-in-Publication Data

Ferrill, Lisa, 1958-
    A far cry from home : life in a shelter for homeless women / Lisa Ferrill.
      p. cm.
    ISBN 0-9622683-6-4 (acid-free paper) : $10.95
    1. Shelters for the homeless—New York (N.Y.) 2. Homeless women—New York (N.Y.) 3. Social work with the homeless—New York (N.Y.)
    I. Title.
    HV4506.N6F47 1991
    362.83'08'6942—dc20   9063431
                                            CIP

Publisher's Note: The relevant facts in this book are real, but names and other identifying details have been changed to protect the privacy of the individuals.

Noble Press books are available in bulk at discount prices. Single copies are available prepaid direct from the Publisher:
Marketing Director
The Noble Press, Inc.
213 W. Institute Place, Suite 508
Chicago, IL 60610

To Dennis

I am only one,
But I am one.
I cannot do everything,
But I can do something.
And because I cannot do everything,
I will not refuse to do the something
that I can do.

Edward Everett Hale
(1822–1909)

Contents

Preface

Broadway plays, exquisite views, tantalizing meals served in plush surroundings . . . New York City, city of luxury, city of thrills.

Lines of people waiting to get into a soup kitchen, men, women, and children panhandling on the street, bodies lying over subway grates to keep warm . . . New York City, city of despair.

Have you ever rushed along the street to be accosted by that nagging feeling of guilt, as you breeze by someone lying in a doorway? Is she alive? Is she ill? Why do we all rush by without finding out if she is all right? Why don't *I* stop?

People sit in train stations, bus stations, parks, doorways, unmistakably sick, with what, I don't know. All are seemingly alone. Some beg. Some don't. Some have open sores that bleed and ooze. Some are drunk. Some talk to themselves or formless others. They have no homes. These are the people that propelled me to finally stop and ask, "Can I help?"

Street people make up a small percentage of the homeless population. Most homeless people blend into the daily flow of urban life. Many families are homeless. Many babies go from the hospital into the shelter system, never knowing what it is like to go home. In this book I have concentrated on that subgroup of homeless individuals whom I have spent the most time with—single women.

Solutions to homelessness are not easily found. But before we can solve problems, we must be sensitive enough to the problems that we create the will to find the solutions. Often, if we do not *feel* the problem, if some emotional response is not elicited, we are not moved to seek solutions. We are often too unmoved to even recognize the questions. In the following pages, I will walk you through some experiences and introduce you to some people I met as a social worker. Hopefully, you will come to feel as I do—that we cannot afford to keep walking by.

⌒Acknowledgments⌒

I would like to give special thanks to my husband, Dennis, whose love and support made this book possible. Many thanks go to my friend Julie Winn, who gave me editorial help and invaluable encouragement. To George Horton and the staff at Catholic Charities Office for the Homeless and Hungry, thank you for the use of the word processor and for moral support along the way. And thank you to all the women without homes that I met, and the scores of volunteers who opened their hearts to them, for enriching my life.

Chapter 1

Who Are These
Women, Anyway?

I always seem to be in a hurry. In New York City time moves half a second faster than its average citizen does. My days are usually filled with appointments in various parts of the city, and much time is spent walking to and from them. I never make it to an appointment without passing a homeless man or woman on the street. And I hurry by.

They bother me, these people. Why are they always around to put a blot on my conscience? Sometimes it is hard to tell if they are alive or dead. And I hurry by. I did not always rush past in anger at the intrusion on my complacent state of mind. It used to be my business to seek these people out, to speak to them, to try to help. Help—that was the snag. How to help? What constituted help? Was it possible to help? These were questions I attempted to answer, often in vain.

I used to be a social worker. After I graduated from the University of Notre Dame in 1980 with a degree in psychology, I took a job as a social worker with Catholic Charities on Long Island, working with homebound elderly people. My annual pay was $9,400. It was frustrating to be the low woman on the totem pole, and my prospects of moving into jobs with greater responsibility were minimal without having an advanced degree. As for my salary, if I had not lived with my parents, I could not have supported myself decently. I was idealistic, but at some point I had to be realistic, too. My father encouraged me to go to graduate school. "You'll be secure then," he would say. "You'll have a profession."

I respected my father for his generally good advice, and I loved him for his unconditional concern for my happiness and wellbeing. He had helped me with major decisions before. It was he who told me he would find a way to send me to Notre Dame after a scholarship I was nominated for fell through. I spent four happy years there. Dad often telephoned my dorm room on Saturday mornings to say hello and to tell me not to study too hard. "Have experiences," he would say. "Life is the best teacher." My father's health began to deteriorate during my freshman year, and when I moved back home with my parents after graduation, he was as often as not in the hospital. An engineer by trade, he had to go on disability and spent much of his energy simply trying to stay alive.

So I applied to a two-year master of social work program at the State University of New York at Stony Brook. It was only forty minutes from home, I liked the community-change focus of the program, and I could afford it with the money I had saved from my job. Part of the curriculum involved fieldwork. During my first year my fieldwork placement concentrated on counseling skills. I was assigned to a local hospital, spending half of the year on the general medical floors and half on the psychiatric wing. In my second year a fieldwork traineeship was offered through the National Institute of Mental Health to research homelessness. I jumped at it.

For several years I had wondered why there were homeless people on the streets in New York City. Who were they? Whenever I went into New York City with friends, I would see these people as I made my way to and from Penn Station, Long Island's gateway to the Big Apple. The first time I saw people sitting or lying on the streets I was startled. What were they doing there? How odd that everyone just rushed by! Yet I allowed myself to go with the flow of the sidewalk traffic and walk by also, not stopping, not speaking, not offering to help. This struck me forcefully because of a Bible passage that had intrigued me since childhood: the parable of the good Samaritan. The parable recounts the story of a man who lies beaten and helpless on the road. Two people walk by without helping; then the third passerby, a Samaritan, stops to help. This story seemed ridiculous to me, unreal. In real life, no one would walk by a man lying on the road, right? At least this seemed rational to *my* mind, who as a child knew nothing but a comfortable, middle-class life in the suburbs with my parents, brother, and sister. Yet here was the same situation. And there I was. And I walked by . . . and walked by. By the time I was in graduate school, I walked by *many* men and women lying on the streets every time I went into the city. But I never knew what to do! I could have just stopped and asked a homeless person if I could help, but I never had the nerve. And it troubled my conscience that a scenario that had once seemed ricidulous to me had now come to life in a very personal, graphic way.

The traineeship offered what could be a first step: researching homelessness. I do not think the professor who was leading the research project had his door beaten down with students applying for the traineeships. Another student and I were awarded them, and we were given stipends and free tuition as well. At the time I entered graduate school, it seemed that homeless people were those largely ignored, depressing bundles lying on the floors of public transportation stations, but by the time I finished graduate school, homelessness had become a field, an area of specialization, a business. It was the spring of 1984, and there were jobs in the field.

Two weeks before I was to graduate, an ad in the help-wanted section of *The New York Times* caught my attention. The ad was for a project director of a private, nonprofit shelter program for homeless women. I sent in my quickly completed resume, and was asked to come in for an interview later that week. When I arrived at the front desk, a well-dressed woman was standing in front of me, asking the receptionist to announce her to Maria. The receptionist sent her upstairs, and then told me to have a seat, as Maria was the woman who was to interview me. I sat nervously in the lobby, imagining that the woman who went up before me would probably get the job. She was older and likely to be more experienced, I conjectured, and she was dressed so much more professionally than I was. After waiting well beyond my appointment time, I was told to go upstairs. Maria apologized to me when I entered her outer office, explaining that she was helping a homeless woman take care of a problem. She brought me to the inner room to introduce her, and to my amazement, it was the woman I had feared was getting the job! When the problem had been resolved and the woman left, I commented to Maria that she was so well dressed. She told me that many of the women were, because we were in a posh part of the city and the quality of the clothing donations reflected that fact. Maria was very personable and had a quick wit. If I got the job, I would report to her, an assistant director of the community center that housed the shelter. I felt very comfortable with Maria, and I certainly wanted the job.

I felt that if I got the job, I would finally be doing something concrete. You cannot get much more basic than shelter. I was idealistic enough to believe it could make a positive difference in people's lives. It was Ralph Nader and Mother Teresa who had helped fuel my idealism. I heard Nader speak during my junior year at Notre Dame, at a time when I was wondering if I should be more pragmatic about money and a "career path." His speech rekindled my idealism as he urged us to follow our hearts and search for ways to contribute to society. I left the auditorium as unclear as ever about exactly what I would do, but I did leave committed to continuing to search for a way to live my life for love, not for money or prestige.

As for Mother Teresa, her call to serve "the poorest of the poor" had rung so true to me. I had admired her for years. She did not preach, she acted. She did not consider the gospel message to "serve the poor" hypothetical; to her it was a truth. And so she served the poor, and she did it with gusto. It was, to me, one of the few truths in life I could find, because it seemed to make some sense out of life. To honor and respect life in any form inherently gave life itself some meaning. I did not want to find myself on my deathbed someday without a clue as to why I had lived. I know of few people for whom Mother Teresa's dedication to aiding the most desperate is not inspirational. Who knows why? I knew I did not have her faith or love, but I could do what little I could do. I decided it was better to contribute whatever drops I had to the pool rather than nothing at all. So I wanted the shelter job very badly – it seemed like it was work that mattered.

Maria told me she would let me know if I made it to the next round of interviews, and I left for Penn Station to catch the train back to Long Island. I did not go all the way back to my apartment in Stony Brook, but got off in Huntington where my parents lived. I had a bad feeling about my father. I called home from the station and found out he had been admitted to the hospital again that afternoon. My father died four days later. I was devastated. I loved him deeply and could not imagine the world without him in it. I felt like part of me died too. I knew I would have to keep extremely busy or I would be overwhelmed by grief. Working with others would help me put my own pain in perspective. The day we buried my father, I received a phone call to come in for the second interview. I graduated that weekend and moved out of my apartment and back in with my mother. I went for the interview the following week, got the job, and began work two weeks later. It was to be the beginning of the most intense period of my life.

———————————————◆———————————————

The organization that hired me was a private, nonprofit social service agency operating out of a settlement house. Built at the turn of the century to meet community needs, the settlement house had retained much of its flavor throughout the years; groups and programs for preschoolers, teens, young adults, senior citizens, and school-age children abounded, lending to its continual profusion of varied sounds and sights. The surrounding neighborhood was one of the richest in Manhattan. Nevertheless, there were large numbers of homeless people in the neighborhood, as there were in almost every New York City neighborhood. What was somewhat unusual, however, was this neighborhood's compassionate response to the homeless people at their doorsteps.

While I was technically employed by the settlement house agency, I was paid ($20,000/year) by a neighborhood coalition of religious institutions. The coalition was established by individuals who wanted to do something to help the homeless people they saw on their streets. This ad hoc group began meeting monthly in church basements in 1979—brainstorming, planning, thinking of ways to raise money. Their first endeavor was to open neighborhood soup kitchens. In short time, they convinced three churches and two synagogues each to operate a lunchtime soup kitchen on a different day of the week, staffed entirely with volunteer labor. As homeless and poor but "domiciled" people quickly filled the soup kitchens, the strengthening coalition searched the neighborhood for a site for a women's shelter. They simultaneously negotiated with religious institutions to open a dinner program for the prospective shelter guests.

The settlement house agency was receptive to housing the shelter, agreeing to provide space and to pay the associated housing and maintenance costs. They would also supervise the project director of the shelter, who would be accountable to the coalition's board of directors as well. The coalition agreed to pay for the shelter personnel and to recruit volunteers to sleep overnight. Nineteen homeless women could be accommodated at the shelter. Housing more than nineteen would mean complying with endless city regulations. With arrangements worked out between the two organizations, the settlement house opened its doors to homeless women in December 1981. Weekday dinner sites were found at five nearby churches, with a synagogue helping out on the weekends. Thus, the impact of this neighborhood's concern began to be felt.

My job description called for me to administer the shelter, supervise the staff, coordinate the dinner program, serve as a liaison with the soup kitchens, screen all new shelter guests, and run a volunteer program. With five dinner sites; five soup kitchen sites; nineteen women needing services; an office overrun with black plastic garbage bags filled with clothes, cartons of canned goods, and bed linens; and a desk abandoned by three employees who had all quit within the past two months, I had my work marching towards me in greeting. It looked like I would have little time for a social life until I got things organized. This would leave me less time to miss my boyfriend, Dennis. He lived in Boston. He had graduated from Harvard Business School a year earlier and now worked for a management consulting firm in Boston. Our opportunities to see each other were already limited, but we would learn to adapt to the new constraints my job imposed. Our relationship was strong.

My first day of work was actually a night. I met Pat, the coalition's board president, at the Monday night dinner site. We met in the church garden, a quaint courtyard between the church and parish house filled with an overgrowth of rambling rose bushes and green ground cover, giving the pleasing appearance of settled disarray. Pat was waiting for me. She spoke with a quiet elegance, and I often had to strain to hear the soft syllables spoken with an authoritative air. We went to the basement of the parish house (I was to see many basements!) where dinner for the shelter guests was being prepared and served by volunteers.

Ready for anything, or so I thought, I was surprised to find a cheerful room, decorated with bright green-and-white bamboo wallpaper, with a subdued group of neat, clean women speaking in hushed tones to each other. Not exactly the disheveled crowd of forbidding characters I had anticipated! I joined one of the two round tables, and shared the delicious meal of chicken, rice, and salad the volunteers had prepared. Not only was the food quite tasty, it was served on dinnerware atop snow-white tablecloths. The women welcomed me with smiles and introductions.

Some of my surprise at seeing this quiet group was a result of my graduate research on homelessness. I had learned that there was about a one-third incidence of mental illness among single homeless people and a somewhat higher percentage for homeless women. However, this group was cordial and interactive, traits not generally associated with "crazy" people, and certainly not with homeless people, because the general public was primarily aware of only those homeless people who slept or begged on the streets. I was to learn that the majority of homeless people were quite different from that stereotypical image. I had already "learned" this during my research, but stigmas and stereotypes dig their roots in deeply, and this would not be the last time I would become aware of some I had not purged from my mind.

Seated to my immediate left was a sweet, gentle woman named Beth. Very frail looking, with almost translucent, wrinkling skin, she still had bright, sparkling eyes. Originally from England, Beth was a lady, very proper and refined, yet warm and sensitive. I was delighted to discover her interest in music, as it has been a love of mine for years. Beth told me she had been a soprano in the opera in her youth. I wondered why she wound up in the shelter, but I did not press her to explain. The meal was one of the few vestiges of a normal life she had, and I did not want to spoil it for her by invading the little privacy she had left. Instead, we chatted about music, favorite composers, musical styles, and so forth.

The meal was ending and there was a relaxed feeling in the

room. I had noticed a piano in a corner of the room and offered to play. Beth came over to sit beside me on the piano bench as I began to play a piece I had composed. When the piece ended, she told me the music had made her feel as if she was part of nature, with a sense of peace and life enveloping her. I was startled and moved by her interpretation of the music because it was the same feeling I myself had while composing it. No one had ever been so in touch with the emotion behind the music before, and I felt a sense of exhilaration at this shared communication. I knew this was bound to be the beginning of an unusual experience. Interesting, fascinating, difficult, depressing, challenging—it grew to be all that and more. There was so much happening all the time, so many new experiences and challenges, so many emotions and concerns, that it is only in looking back that I begin to absorb it more fully.

Pat and I left the dinner site to go to the shelter, a ten-minute walk away. I mentioned my surprise at how quiet and polite everyone had been. "Well, they are not always like that," Pat said. "The women seemed to be on their best behavior tonight because they were meeting you for the first time. We have had some incidents of violence," she warned, "so it is not as rosy as it may seem." I tossed off her warning, sure that I could handle whatever came along.

I was so anxious to try to help these people that I felt I could conquer anything. I was sick of seeing suffering human beings on the streets, and I knew that for every homeless person I saw, there were scores of less visible homeless people who were likewise in desperate circumstances. I wanted to be part of a solution to this societal dilemma. But I had hoped the solutions would be whole. Instead, I found myself becoming part of a partial solution to homelessness, which proved to be an incredibly draining experience. Whole solutions cannot become a reality unless society as a whole feels the problem, and works together on the solutions. But that is getting ahead of my story.

We arrived at the shelter as the maintenance men were setting up the beds in the settlement house auditorium. Since the auditorium was used as a special education classroom in the morning, an after-school recreation room in the afternoon, and an adult education program room in the evening, the beds had to be set up every night by 10 P.M. when the women were allowed in and removed by 8 A.M. when the schoolchildren arrived. It was quite a routine, and the maintenance men often complained about this labor-intensive task.

Fifteen beds were set up along the periphery of the rectangular room, with four beds set up in the center. There was a small auditorium stage with four lockers in one corner of it. One large locker contained fresh bed linens and towels; the other three were used by the women to store their personal things. A small room adjacent to the auditorium entrance was converted into a lounge area each night. The lounge contained a portable television, a few chairs, and a small table with a reading light for the overnight aide. The aide was a nonprofessional staffperson paid to stay awake and supervise the shelter all night. A recent high school graduate who lived in the neighborhood currently held this position on weeknights; a sixty-year-old man who worked for a home run by a religious order during the week held the position on weekends.

Next to the lounge area was the volunteers' room: a shabby, converted classroom with two beds in it. The volunteers slept here to provide supplemental coverage in case of an emergency. Supplies were also kept in this room, such as the coffee urn, shampoo, soap, first-aid kit, and an assortment of other, sundry items. I surveyed everything, making mental notes of which areas to attack first to make things neater and better organized.

Pat continued the tour, leading me down a long, L-shaped staircase outside the lounge area. A windowless laundry room was at the base of the stairs. The air was stale, thick with odors from old clothes, shoes, laundry detergent, and the overused dryer. The washer, dryer, and three walls of various types of shelves and closets filled the room. The three closets were fairly large, with one of the closets reserved for donations. The women had to share the remaining two closets, which once again afforded no privacy. Makeshift shelves lined two of the walls, each overflowing with bags, boxes, and articles of clothing. Plastic garbage bags brimming with belongings were stuffed into every conceivable cranny in the room, alongside bulging brown boxes overflowing with rolled-up clothing, magazines, boots, and umbrellas; odds and ends were strewn about haphazardly. Everything looked broken, dirty, tattered beyond repair, flowing into everything else in one big communal mess. This room held all the belongings of the nineteen women: the remnants of their former lives.

"Onward," Pat said, and we took a quick look into the "men's" shower room, which served as the homeless women's shower area at night. The shelter guests used the men's shower area rather than the women's, because the men's shower was a large, communal shower, which the maintenance staff thought was easier to clean than the separate shower stalls in the women's area. Since there were no men in the building after 10 P.M. who might use the shower facilities, the decision had been made to open only the men's shower for the shelter guests. I tried to imagine what it would feel like to have to shower with a bunch of strangers, to have to shower with anyone at all! Later I was to learn that since all the women preferred to shower in privacy, they took turns using the shower room. That meant waiting in line before showering and ultimately going to bed, but apparently it was worth it for this little bit of privacy.

It was time for the women to come in. The aide opened the auditorium doors that led to the street, and the women poured in, the same ones I had seen at the dinner plus a few others who did not go to the meal. Each woman immediately went to her bed. The beds were not assigned formally, but I was to learn that each woman quickly established a "turf," staking out a bed and the surrounding area. It seemed to provide the women with some sense of order in this otherwise chaotic existence.

The women went to the lockers behind the stage to get their linens and belongings, made up their own beds, and then moved either towards the shower room or towards the lounge for tea, coffee, and cookies. The room was alive with activity and constant motion, but it was a tired motion, a motion heavy with effort and visible pain, as elderly, sick and exhausted women dragged bags and bodies about the room. I smiled when greeting them and tried to remember which names belonged to the faces I had met shortly before.

A young woman, Kathy, came over to talk to me by the snack tables. She was about thirty-five years old, with shoulder-length, coarse, blonde hair, a small woman with a slight build. At first I could not place what seemed a bit strange about her physical appearance. Then I realized that she was missing several of her top front teeth. Missing teeth were to become a common sight to me for the simple reason that poor people cannot afford dental care. Despite the missing teeth, Kathy had a pleasant smile, which softened my lonely twinge of being new on the job in this barren, drab environment. Kathy told me how happy she was that I had been hired because they needed a social worker to help them get out of the shelter. Her sense of eager anticipation touched me as she kissed me lightly on the cheek before she began her nightly ritual of settling in.

It truly was a ritual, because for each woman there was so much involved before finally going to sleep. There were linens to find, a bed to make, bags to unload, nightclothes, shampoo, and other items to find before showering, possibly a load of wash to do—all before collapsing for six or seven hours before the aide woke everyone up at 6 A.M. The auditorium had to be cleared by 7 A.M. so that the maintenance men could begin cleaning the room and setting it up as a classroom again.

One woman's labors seemed particularly elaborate on this night. Actually, she was doing the work for two. Jean was forty-eight and her mother, Lily, eighty-four; both stayed at the shelter but did not go to the dinner program. Jean had a heart-shaped face with clear, porcelainlike skin, in which were set round, dark eyes that looked sad and weary. Her brow appeared to be permanently furrowed with worry lines, and her hair was pulled back neatly in a bun. Lily was hunched over, dependent on Jean for support when walking. She had a deeply lined face and steel-gray hair pulled on top of her head in a loose bun. Both women were neatly and immaculately dressed, as they would be every day of the sixteen months I would see them at the shelter.

Jean had pulled two beds together to form one, and had seated her mother in a chair before gathering washing materials in a small basin. She then went downstairs to the men's bathroom, which none of the other women used, and began scrubbing one of the toilets and surrounding area. Later that week, when I spent the entire night in the shelter, I learned that this scrubbing was only the beginning of a nightly ritual that took Jean until 3 or 4 A.M. to complete.

After scrubbing the bathroom, she would then bring her mother downstairs, give her a complete sponge bath, wash her hair, put on her nightclothes, scrub their plastic bed coverings, put on the linens, and put her mother to bed. Jean would then go back to the basement and give herself a sponge bath and shampoo, and then wash their clothing by hand because she thought she did a better job than the washing machine could do. By the time all of this was accomplished, it was usually at least 3 A.M. Since everyone had to be up by 6 A.M., this left very little time for her to sleep, but she chose to sacrifice sleeping time rather than lower her accustomed standard of cleanliness.

Upstairs everything seemed to be going smoothly, except for the troubles of one woman who also had not been at dinner. Leslie was a white-haired, neatly groomed woman of sixty who was talking in rather filthy language to an imaginary foe. Yelling at the foe might be putting it more aptly. No one seemed to notice, or at least no one was paying attention to her. When I asked the aide what the problem was, she said that Leslie did this every single night, sometimes louder and longer than others. Everyone was used to it.

"You filthy bastard. Get your fucking hands off of me! Communist spy! You look like Jesus Christ Himself!" she shouted to a space of air above her bed, hovering near it, jolting away, hovering, jolting, hovering, jolting.

Communists. Jesus Christ. Two common themes I was to hear repeatedly by those suffering from mental illness—government and religion.

I wondered with amusement at what was going on across the room. Situated in the bed next to Kathy's was a colorful menage of confusion: an obese woman creating a flurry of activity, a black angora cat in a baby carriage, colorful bags of purple and hot pink, and brightly colored quilted bed coverings. This was Jackie.

With Jackie, chaos always reigned. She had the ability to make you love her while simultaneously driving you to madness with her penchant for creating havoc. The cat was Danny.

"Hi. How do you like the place?" Jackie asked, as I walked over to her bed. "Have you met Danny? He's my baby. Most spoiled cat in New York, only he thinks he's a person, don't you, Danny?" The cat lay lazily amongst baby blankets in his carriage, well-groomed, well-fed, and seemingly quite content with his life, indifferent to all but Jackie.

"He's adorable. I'm surprised he's allowed in here," I remarked.

"Well, they made an exception in his case, seeing as he's so well-kept and all, and I've had him for so long," she said. "I'm glad you're here, but I'm sorry Katie left." Katie was one of the former social workers and the backbone of the shelter. "We loved Katie. She was a lot of fun. We had a good time together." She chuckled, remembering happy moments.

Filling Katie's shoes was not going to be easy. Although Katie had not been the project director, all the women respected her a great deal and would measure me against her rather than the former project director. Gaining the respect and trust of the women would be paramount in being able to run a smoothly operating shelter and in helping the women move *out* of it. I had met Katie once. She was bubbly and effervescent, with energy to spare. I am a more quiet person, less "fun" than Katie; time and hard work would have to win their trust.

It was now well past 11 P.M. My first whole day of work would begin tomorrow. The next train to Long Island was at midnight, enough time for me to get the subway to Penn Station where the Long Island Rail Road (LIRR) is. I said goodnight to everyone and walked five blocks to the subway station, my mind trying to sort through the shelter setup and the panorama of people I had met.

The subway was well-lit, and I had to wait only about five minutes for the train. As there was no direct route to Penn Station, I rode for less than ten minutes, then had to change to another train, and finally to a third train for the last ten blocks. I made it to the LIRR with only minutes to spare. I was tense from riding alone at that hour and trying to find the right connections. Realizing the commute was going to be more troublesome than I had anticipated, I made myself comfortable for the seventy-minute ride to Huntington, where I would drive my waiting car the last fifteen minutes home. I told myself that this was only temporary: I had moved in with my mother just for the summer to help her get used to the idea of living without my father. If nothing else, the long train ride gave me time to think and relax. My thoughts often ran to my father, and I would cry quietly in my seat on the train ride home, thinking about the cycle of life, a cycle that had ended for my father and in so many ways seemed just to be beginning for me. But what did the cycle hold for these women?

Chapter 2

No Room at the Inn

♦

During my first three weeks at work I felt like a bad magician, continuously shuffling and reshuffling the deck of things that needed to be done. I tried to prioritize, but everything was a priority. Many of the women had dropped by my office during my first week, each with a story more desperate than the last. The women who did not come seemed in even greater need, either too mentally disturbed, fearful, or without hope to come for help. On top of this, there were linens that *had* to be ordered, breakfast food that *had* to be there, volunteers that *had* to be scheduled each night, new staffpeople that *had* to be interviewed, and countless homeless women who called or came by in the hopes of getting a bed. These women *had* to be attended to as well, for it was too heart-wrenching just to say, "We have no room" and turn away. These women were usually in agony when they made contact with the shelter, so I tried to find them a bed in another shelter (no easy task), sometimes fed them a bit, and gave those who needed it transportation money out of our emergency relief fund, so a woman could get to the shelter that had a bed for her.

Unless I had an available bed, I hated getting those "walk-ins" or "phone-ins." There was no time limit for how long a woman could stay at the shelter; consequently, turnover was low. Most women stayed until they found a permanent living situation, and this was literally taking years. Sometimes a bed would become available due to a prolonged hospitalization; sometimes a woman would simply disappear; others had to be asked to leave. All in all, there was an average of two free beds per month. I got an average of two calls per *day* from homeless women and social workers begging for a bed.

When a hospital social worker called, or a worker from another shelter or agency seeking a bed for someone they could not accommodate, it was not so bad to tell them I did not have a bed. That is, it did not *feel* so bad, because I was already removed from the woman actually wanting the bed. But when a homeless woman called on her own, it was hell. There was no buffer, no psychological hiding place—there was just a desperate woman and me, and more often than not I would have to tell her no.

Calls would come at all hours of the day and night. Night calls were the worst. If a woman called late at night, I knew she did not have many options. I could not send her to other agencies or call around for a bed, because intake was only opened during the day at private shelters. She had one of two options: to go to one of the two twenty-four-hour drop-in centers for women or to go to a city shelter. Most of the women I met were too scared of the city shelters to go there. Huge warehouses of sick and desperate people, these shelters were often too intimidating to venture into, and the fear of violence ran high. The fear of getting to the central intake office, located in a dismal part of the city, also prevented some women from taking this option. The drop-in centers were less threatening, but they only provided chairs to sit in all night. Some women chose this option, but more often than not, the despairing person on the other end of my "no" would opt for a night riding the subways, sitting in an all night coffee shop, or on the street, rather than attempt to deal with the city shelter system.

I would try to soften my "no." I knew these women were flailing for a lifeline, a lifeline I did not have. Sometimes the woman would cry and tell me her story, just because she needed someone to talk to, and I would listen and wish her well. When I hung up the phone, I would wonder what would happen to this solitary woman I had left with no tangible hope. Sometimes it was harder to say no than others. Sometimes the woman would beg or plead with me, trying to squeeze a bed out of what she must have perceived to be a hard heart. These entreaties remained with me, floating to the fore of my consciousness every once in a while, a nagging reminder of all those with whom I had severed the connection.

The feelings stirred by having to reject women filled with fear and pain were brutal. In everyday life, you generally do not run into people who are pleading with you to help them with a life-or-death situation. Perhaps life or death is a bit too strong. Oddly enough, people *do* survive on the street. However, just surviving is not my idea of life, so when I could not help a desperate woman, I felt it. One can only become immune to so much pain.

Sometimes my endurance gave way. I spent several nights sleeping at the shelter during those first few weeks so that I could understand the women and the shelter operation better. The project director was allowed to sleep in the agency's staff lounge on the sixth floor. An intercom phone was hooked up from the first-floor shelter to this sixth-floor room. It was very gloomy in that lounge. It felt eerie to be isolated from the only other people in the darkened building. The dimly lit room held a hospital bed in front of the curtainless window, an easy chair, and a broken television. I would make up the bed with shelter sheets and sleep in my clothes for the five or six hours I might be up there. I never slept well on that plastic-covered mattress, with the orange-tinted street light making the room seem even dingier. There was a heaviness, an oppressive silence in the building, punctuated every now and then by one of the more disturbed women calling out in the night.

One night at the end of June, I came upstairs to get my bed ready, feeling depressed and hollow. It had not been a good day — the submersion into a world of daily suffering, the sense that I could never get on top of all the work there was to do, the unending flow of people in anguish, the summer heat. I wanted to cry but tried to sleep. Then the phone rang; it was 11:45 P.M. My heart sank as I picked up the phone to hear a woman begging for a bed. We were full, with one bed being saved for Stacie, who was in the hospital and expected to return any day.

The woman on the phone, Lucille, was calling from a street corner in Harlem. Her landlord had inexplicably locked her out of her single room in the single room occupancy (SRO) hotel where she lived. This problem was not uncommon: landlords often ruthlessly and unjustifiably evicted people in order to get higher rents, or to warehouse the building, so that once emptied it could be sold to a real estate developer at a sizable profit. Lucille cried pitifully, telling me how frightened she was at the prospect of having no place to go. I could not take it. The day had been quite draining, and I did not have the strength to say no again. I said yes.

There was a risk involved in accepting someone over the phone at that time of night. If the person appeared to be a threat of any kind when she showed up, or if she was drunk or using drugs, I would be faced with having to ask her to leave. The woman would have wasted her time and effort and would be that much more exhausted and desperate. Then again, if she refused to leave, I would be in a more vulnerable position, because the rest of the building was deserted and the other women might be disturbed. My instincts told me that Lucille was a good bet. I was worried, though, that when Stacie came back from the hospital, Lucille might not want to give the bed back to her without being forced to do so. Lucille might very well have to go to the city shelter after all, and I wondered if it made sense to postpone this by having accepted her for just a night or two.

Fortunately, it all worked out, because Stacie's hospital stay had to be extended for a few weeks due to unexpected medical complications. That gave Lucille time to try to rent a cheap room somewhere while she looked for domestic work. She could not find a room and was having difficulty getting job references, which ultimately meant she could not find a job. Determined to get out of the shelter whatever way she could, Lucille wound up enrolling in a city college program and rented a room without heat or hot water using a school loan. She was sixty years old.

A large percentage of the women who came to the shelter were senior citizens. Seven out of nineteen of the initial "group" were over sixty years of age, not including Lucille. Five of those seven were over seventy years old. I was surprised. To be homeless was hard enough. To be homeless and old . . . !

Emma's circumstances were the most pathetic . She came to the shelter when it first opened, one and a half years earlier. Her eyesight was poor then, but it was getting worse daily. It was now obvious that this seventy-nine-year-old woman was virtually blind, but Emma refused to accept this fact and therefore refused to accept medical attention. She could see shadows well enough to navigate to her bed in the shelter successfully, but she needed help getting her linens, bathing, and eating. By day, she would sit outside on the steps leading to the shelter. Rain or shine, Emma would be huddled in the corner of the stoop, with her wizened face and cloudy, squinted eyes, cheerfully saying hello to those who greeted her as they walked by.

Emma told me her story one early July morning when I joined her on the steps. Her face mapped the beauty of age, deeply creviced wrinkles creating a sort of maze, like a knot in an old tree trunk. She had few teeth, leaving her mouth sunken into the curve of her protruding chin. Her eyes were light blue, squinted shut, her hair snow white and closely cropped. A small woman, she wore several layers of clothing to protect herself from the elements.

It was easy to engage Emma in conversation. I told her I wanted to help her in whatever way I could, and the story rapidly unfolded. Emma was a nurse for over twenty-five years at a hospital a few blocks away from the shelter. She used to live alone in an apartment in the neighborhood until she was mugged while going into the building. At this point, it began to become difficult to discern fantasy from fact in her narrative.

Emma was mentally alert and conversant on many subjects. However, it became apparent that she became somewhat confused about certain subjects. The hard part was trying to determine where the confusion began and ended.

Emma told me that Nancy, another old woman in the shelter, had been behind the mugging. The way for me to help her, she said, was to keep Nancy away from her, because she was always spying on her and planning another attack (Nancy could barely walk a half block without a mishap, let alone attack someone). I tried to keep Emma focused on reality, but once she got sidetracked, it was hard to stop her. Emma loved to talk, once she got going, and it was actually quite fascinating to witness her in action, weaving reality and fantasy together in an effortless web.

After an hour of talk, all I knew was that she had once lived in that apartment, which might or might not have still been rented for her use. Emma claimed that the rent was still being paid by her two nephews, who were in charge of her finances and lived out of state.

However, the likelihood that the rent was still being paid seemed minute, judging from the fact that Emma also said she had not been in touch with her nephews for almost two years, did not want to contact them presently, and so on. Emma was too scared, at any rate, to live in an apartment alone. She would not consider getting household help for fear the person would harm her, would not consider going to a rest home for the elderly, would not consider getting medical attention for her eyes, would not go to the meal program or the senior center two doors away, and merely wanted me to get Nancy away from her.

Emma said she loved sitting outdoors in the fresh air and was doing fine eating whatever passersby gave her. Of course, she had very strong opinions about what each shelter guest's problem was, and what each one needed to do to get out. She then warned me to be careful, because I "seemed like a nice girl," and the former worker, Katie, had been poisoned and coerced into leaving the shelter.

With the limited time I had for each woman, and all my administrative responsibilities, I knew I needed help with this one. I enlisted several volunteers who expressed particular concern for Emma, and decided we should all try to focus on one problem of the myriad she had. We decided to focus our efforts on her eyesight, because one of our volunteers, a nurse whose husband was an eye specialist, advised us that Emma's eyesight could probably be improved with proper medical care. Each day, a volunteer would stop by the steps and talk to Emma, trying to give her support and encouragement, trying to help her realize that she would remain blind without help. Others helped her bathe and washed her clothes at night in the shelter. I called a special agency for the blind, and they said they would send a worker to the steps to talk to Emma and encourage her to accept help. We hoped that with time, patience, and care, she would trust us enough to allow us to help her. With relatively little effort, we were able to get Emma to eat dinner regularly.

On July 1, the dinner program host sites closed their doors until after Labor Day. Dinners during the summer were to be prepared at the settlement house under my "supervision"—a gross understatement. When summer rolls around in New York City, everyone who can afford to leave does. It is hot and humid. Most of the volunteers came from the well-to-do neighborhood surrounding the shelter, and were either homemakers with grown children or working women. These volunteers were now either at their summer homes or could not leave work early enough to prepare the meal at the shelter.

So every weeknight, the nineteen shelter guests were left with me, and I had very little cooking experience, no culinary talents, and no time. What an experience! Cooking a meal meant having the groceries to prepare it. Since we had only a small refrigerator, with a half-broken freezer that took pleasure in forming daily icebergs, I had to go to the corner food store every day to buy enough food for dinner. I got a kick out of this. The checkout people would wonder at me, buying two gallons of milk, four loaves of bread, three heads of lettuce, five pounds of chopped meat, and so on, each day.

The kitchen was down the hall from my office on the third floor, approximately five feet by six feet, with no windows or ventilation. To say that it was sweltering does not do it justice. No more than two people could move around in it at one time. The elevator in the building was old, unreliable, and got stuck at least once a week. We did not use it at night because if it did get stuck, help might not come until morning. (One night, the aide was particularly tired and rode in it, getting stuck for five hours.) After cooking the meal, we had to carry it down three flights of stairs to the shelter. Never in my life had I had so much exercise.

The first week of this new cooking arrangement included the Fourth of July. The agency's executive director, Paul, suggested having a barbecue for the women on the third-floor roof deck. I thought he was joking.

"You want me to have a barbecue for nineteen homeless women on the roof? What if someone decides to jump?" I was caught again in stereotypes.

"Do it. It will be nice for them," he said. On July 4, after spending the day on Long Island with my family, I took the train in, carrying four dozen frozen hamburger patties in a shopping bag.

I did not want to work that night. Holidays were always celebrated in a big way at my parents' home, and it bred in me the expectation of family and fun. I left my family and their friends barbecuing in the backyard next to the built-in swimming pool. The day was sunny and hot. I was full of self-pity when I rounded the corner of the shelter. Clustered on the shelter steps were all the women, looking forlorn, dejected, and depressed. Oh God. So many mixed emotions. I struggled to overcome my selfishness and depression, and tried to muster a cheerful attitude.

It felt strange to be preparing to barbecue on a roof with a group of homeless women on the Fourth of July. It was so out of the realm of my experience. But it was, at second thought, just a barbecue with some women who shared the same holiday as I did. "Homeless"—it was that label that obscured the core reality, that made it seem strange somehow to have the barbecue. It was the label that distanced me psychologically; the label gave me the illusion that they were somehow different from me, that I could be removed. The realization and belief that we were all quite the same began to sink in on that rooftop. These women, too, longed for celebration, for companionship, for warmth. The label could only obscure our shared humanity if there were no human contact between us. Contact shattered the myth of difference by holding up a mirror of humanity.

I started the charcoal, and brought out the salads, soda, and snacks I had purchased the day before. Some of the women helped to set up, and it began to look more like a party. I tended to the coals, thinking of all the Fourth of Julys my father had done the same task. Jean and Lily were standing nearby. Jean was private, very polite, with a rigid demeanor. We began speaking of food, and the conversation eventually led to what had brought her and her mother to the shelter.

Jean's father had been ill and was hospitalized for months. One day, returning from a visit to the hospital, they found themselves locked out of their apartment, an eviction notice tacked to the door. Jean did not understand why they had been evicted and felt that their landlord was doing something illegal, but she did not know how to fight it.

Jean and Lily then came to the shelter, visiting the hospital daily until the father died. I told Jean I was sorry, and that I had just lost my father, too. "No one has helped us," she said. I suggested she come to my office that week so that we could try to figure out a plan for them. Jean eagerly accepted the offer. We continued talking as we tended the coals, and Jean told me a little of what it was like growing up and going to boarding school in a convent in Poland. Her family came to the United States shortly after World War II ended, and she had cared for her parents ever since. She had never held a job outside of the home and had never married. Lily had a married daughter living in Connecticut, but Jean said she was not able to help them financially and that her family was already crowded in their small home.

I felt sorrow for them. The loss of Lily's husband/Jean's father, the loss of a home, the loss of dignity in their lives—I strained to imagine how they felt. I could barely contain my own sorrow at losing my father, without adding the loss of home and everyday decency. I marveled at their strength.

The burgers tasted good, and we strained to see fireworks set off from a distant building as the stars began to come out. Freedom, independence, the American dream. The hot summer air hung in a bittersweet shroud as each woman became absorbed in her own thoughts while looking up at the sky.

◆

It was difficult to spend the time I wanted to with Jean, Lily, and the rest of the women, because the flow simply never stopped. Two mornings after the barbecue, I arrived at work at 9 A.M. to the receptionist, Laverne's, indifferent "She's for you." Thud. Not first thing in the morning! But there she was, a walk-in. Many women came in person to ask for a bed, knowing it was harder for someone to turn them away in person than over the phone, hoping there was room for one more. Saying no over the phone was bad enough; saying no in person was an emotional jar each and every time. Removing myself, keeping a "professional distance"—these were skills my heart did not seem to learn, as it reminded me that this was another human being with the same physical and emotional needs as myself, and I could not help her. I would try to comfort myself by saying I was doing what I could. My inner voice would prod, "There has got to be more." I tried to shake off my usual morning fogginess and put on my emotional armor. I had no bed for this woman.

The woman, Megan, appeared to be in her twenties. She was well groomed, rather composed, and sitting amongst eight very large boxes and suitcases. I went over to her and began to ask some very basic questions, but only received quizzical looks. I thought she must speak a foreign language, but was startled to learn, through a quickly scribbled note, that Megan was deaf and mute. This was a tough one. After an exchange of jottings, I learned that an organization for deaf people had sent this recently evicted young woman to me. I immediately called them, furious that they would send Megan and all her belongings directly to the shelter without first checking for an empty bed, or at the very least, explaining her situation. Such shoddy and irresponsible work was sickening to witness, but it was clear, after speaking with them, that there would be no help from their end.

After futile attempts at private shelters, I wound up putting this disabled woman in a taxi, with all her boxes and bags, and sending her to the city shelter system, where her communication problems could only be compounded by this large, bureaucratic maze. At least I knew the city shelter system would take her. A court order upheld that shelter was every citizen's right, and that the city was obliged to provide such shelter, if necessary. This was small solace as I watched the overburdened taxi shuttle this frightened and confused woman to a begrudging environment, where she would be an easy target for abuse, where her disability would make it even harder for her to demand help from the skeletal social work staff.

I felt as if I had just helped her die. She was so sweet, so innocent. I felt a rush of life, a rush of death. How many other women, equally sweet and innocent, perhaps hostile and bitter, how many human beings in equal need had I turned away? How many went to other shelters? How many went to the subways? streets? parks? to men who would beat them again? How many are still left to scream in the night, while we sleep safely and soundly in our beds? . . . soundly?

Chapter 3

Going Over the Edge

◆

After a week of listening to complaints about the preparation and selection of what I cooked for dinner, I realized I was going about it all wrong. I was trying to mother nineteen grown women. It suddenly became obvious that the whole program, from staff to volunteers, was operating in a maternal mode. In our desire to help we were doing all the concrete things we possibly could for the women, all the things you could put your hands on, like cooking and cleaning. What we needed was less of that and more helping by encouraging the women to help themselves, helping them to realize what they were and could be capable of.

To this end, a new dinner program plan was devised. I divided up the various tasks, such as menu planning, setting and clearing the table, cooking, and cleaning the kitchen. That night at the shelter, I held the first of many "community meetings," explaining the new system and the reasons why I was putting it into effect. I entreated the women to volunteer for the tasks with which they felt most comfortable. With the exception of Emma, and one or two others who were not presently able to do a task, we had duties assigned to everyone.

The results were remarkable. It took some pushing at times, but for the most part the women seemed to enjoy their new responsibilities. In fact I had to reiterate the philosophy of the program to some of the volunteers: in their efforts to help, they took over certain tasks and offended some of the women. Several women became possessive and proud of their roles. Beth buzzed around the tiny kitchen every night, washing the dishes and putting everything in order. She loved it. "Makes me feel useful," she would say, singing as she scrubbed the pots.

I realized that doing basic household tasks allowed several former homemakers to do what they had gotten a sense of satisfaction from before becoming homeless. Sometimes I would feel like doing something myself in an effort to save time or confusion, but I restrained myself as I saw the rewards of letting people do for themselves, and the danger of fostering a sense of helplessness and dependency by taking away that opportunity. The atmosphere changed from a parent/child feeling to one of group cooperation— not perfect by any means, but greatly improved. I still did the shopping and most of the cooking because many of the older or disabled women had a hard time making it up the three flights of stairs to the kitchen. But as the summer wore on, several new volunteers were recruited who were able to help prepare the meals.

I felt good about the changes and looked forward to the day when we would have additional staffpeople who could concentrate their efforts on working with the women towards moving out of the shelter. Each woman generally had so many problems that it was not just a matter of finding an affordable roof. There might be physical and/or mental health problems, financial entitlement complications, employment difficulties, drug or alcohol addiction, the basic problem of finding housing in a city that caters more and more to the very wealthy, and a vast number of minor problems, collectively forming a constellation of pressing needs. And trying to convince women overcome by fear or depression to accept help was often the biggest obstacle of all.

Finding staffpeople was not easy. I was looking for one staffperson to start in the summer and another to start in the fall when we opened our day program. Maria, my supervisor, was off for the month of July, during which time I reported to her boss, Paul, the settlement house agency's executive director. At his insistence, the schedule for the new staffperson was to be 3 to 11 P.M., Wednesday through Friday, and 5 P.M. to 9 A.M., Saturday/Sunday—salary, $13,500. I thought this was insane, but after voicing my objections and being overruled, I had no choice but to try to find this saint.

I got a handful of resumes and interviewed all that seemed plausible. Like clockwork, as the interviewees heard the salary, they said things to the effect of "You must be joking." I did not blame them. It was hard enough to find people who were interested in working with homeless people because of all the stigmas attached, besides asking them to work an awkward shift including two overnight stays on the weekend, all for a subsistence-level salary.

I did get one Protestant minister, female, who was interested enough to tell me she would think about it. I barely had time to hope when I got the call: "I decided to take a job in Connecticut. It's more involved with a congregation, and it pays better." She was my last hope. I felt drained; I was working more overtime than I ever bothered to count. Each day of work was like hiking up a mountain whose summit was always as far away as when I took my first step. And the summer sizzled on.

August had begun. August in New York City is uncomfortably humid. The humidity, combined with the exhaust of the incredible number of cars, buses, and trucks that daily jam the streets of Manhattan, creates a thick air that seems to crawl over one's body. It is not pleasant, to say the least. August is a quiet month in Manhattan. Many working people take their vacations in August, and with that group went several more volunteers. Thanks to the loyalty and devotion of a core group, we got by.

After the minister rejected the job offer, I went to Paul's office to tell him the bad news.

"Well, you will just have to keep looking," he said.

"No," I found myself saying. "We will never fill this position. No older worker with a family will take it because of the hours. No young person will take this position because it ruins their weekends and social life. No one will take it for this money when there are other jobs out there that are paying more and are generally much more attractive in terms of working conditions. The only person who would take this job is either a saint or a total loser who can't get a job anywhere else. We have to change the hours."

After a lengthy discussion, it was agreed that since an overnight aide was on seven nights a week it was not essential that the program assistant we were seeking work on the weekends. (I usually did not work the weekends either, although I was always on call for emergencies.) We set the hours for 3 to 11 P.M., Monday through Friday, with the understanding that the schedule was to be flexible on an as-needed basis. A new ad was placed in *The New York Times* and I crossed my fingers.

Meanwhile, I was getting to know the women fairly well, and I felt we had developed a mutual respect. There was one woman, though, whom I was wary of. There were signs that she might become violent. It was like being at the mouth of an active volcano; I hoped the rumblings I sensed below would not come to the surface.

Norma had come to the shelter about seven months before I was hired. She had been in the psychiatric unit of a local hospital when I started, and we had held her bed for her in accordance with shelter policy. Without this policy, a woman in our shelter might not seek treatment because she would have to worry about finding a new shelter to stay in when she got out of the hospital. With only a handful of private shelters for women, this would probably have meant that the woman would have to go into the city shelter system or else stay on the street, either option provoking understandable fear and resistance.

Sometime in early May, Katie had persuaded Norma to voluntarily admit herself to the hospital. Norma's delusions of strange beings gnawing at her stomach had become so pervasive that she could no longer stand the consequent psychological pain and finally sought relief. She had been back at the shelter for several weeks now, after spending about six weeks in the hospital. Initially she appeared to be free from the psychological torture, but that soon changed.

There was very sketchy information scribbled in Norma's file stating that she was currently on parole for stabbing her former employer. Although he was stabbed several times, he did not die. Norma spent time in prison. Such an act of violence seemed totally incongruous, judging from her pleasant demeanor. She was a very attractive woman, about fifty years old, with an appealing German accent and a well-groomed appearance she took pains to preserve. Her carefully coiffed salt-and-pepper hair crowned her delicate facial features, and she wore bright, fashionable clothing with a feminine, elegant air.

I barely had a chance to become familiar with this woman with the ready smile before she began to decompensate, as psychologists say, or to go out of her mind, as a layman might say. Norma began to have trouble sleeping at night. John, one of the aides, reported that she sat up with him for most of the night, rocking her body back and forth on the chair and muttering angrily about the government or sex. She was being seen by a psychiatrist on an outpatient basis, but did not want to take the drugs prescribed for her because she blamed them for "causing [her] stomach to get eaten up." Since it is against the law to force anyone to take prescribed drugs, or to see a doctor, we had no choice but to watch the mental torture gradually but forcefully take hold of Norma once again. The mental health laws, which many years ago were criticized for being too restrictive, have swung to the other extreme. It is now often impossible to get help for someone unless she/he is suicidal or homicidal. And it is not easy to prove either of those two things, as I found out.

The continuum of mental health, or mental illness (depending on how you choose to label it), places optimal health on one end, neurosis somewhere in between, and psychosis on the other end. Psychosis is when an individual loses touch with reality in a big way, and Norma was headed in that direction fast. She began to fantasize about Paul, who stopped in to see how the shelter was doing fairly regularly. John reported that she sat in a snack room chair and talked to herself throughout the night, describing lurid sexual encounters she was going to have with Paul. This progressed to delusions about killing Paul for betraying her by having sex with his wife. Norma chanted, "I will kill him, I will kill him," in rhythm with her rocking, with an occasional interjection about how people were murdered and tortured during World War II.

My growing concern was that she would completely snap one night and try to harm herself or someone in the shelter. I tried to weigh the real possibility of a threat against the option of throwing her out on the street, which is essentially what I would be doing if I asked her to leave. No private shelter would take her in her present condition, and she would never go to the city, "government," shelter. I waited and I watched, carefully.

I did not have to wait long. I was called to the main floor one afternoon by Laverne, who said Norma wanted to see me. Ever polite and cordial, Norma began speaking in hushed tones of needing help.

"I have a problem, you see, it is not something I like to speak of. I was at the clinic, you see, because the fucking bastards told me I have a problem, I want you to know."

She started to get louder and more agitated. She had said peculiar things before, but then I had known there was no imminent danger of her getting trapped in her internal world. I had known by the *way* she said things more than by the actual content of what she said that she still maintained a grip on reality. Now, there was something radically different in the way Norma was speaking. She was standing at the front desk, where a dozen or so people from other programs were milling around.

"Don't you understand what I'm saying?" she suddenly shrieked. "I have fucking syphilis!"

The intensity with which she said this was alarming. I asked her to come to my office where we would have more privacy. She complied and seemed to calm down for a few moments as we walked up the three flights of stairs.

"Okay, Norma, tell me what happened," I said, as my mind raced ahead, trying to think of the right things to say and to determine how I should react to her. I did not have much time to compose myself. Within one minute, Norma's voice, anger, and explosiveness had escalated to a level I had never witnessed before, even though I had spent considerable time working on psychiatric wards. Norma's face seemed to have outgrown her skin; her neck was so taut that it looked as though her blood vessels would come spilling out. Her body lunged toward my desk in a hostile knot as she banged her fist on it, screaming, "My cunt! My cunt! They have taken my cunt and given me syphilis! Do you know what that means? The JEWS!! They have killed all the Jews," she hissed now, spitting out the words as if they would choke her if she held them in a millisecond longer.

For the first time I knew what it meant to be out of your mind: you can talk crazy, you can act crazy, but I had always seen some thread of sanity. This time I could not, and my body reacted by pumping adrenaline. I could see that Norma could misperceive my smallest gesture as a threat and then turn all her hostility on me.

"I'll be right back," I told her, and raced down a flight of stairs to Paul's office.

"Norma's going crazy in my office!" I blurted out.

"What do you mean?"

"I think she is having a psychotic break," I said. "I'm afraid she is going to get violent."

Paul said he would call her psychiatrist. He had tried to fill the gap between the time the former project director had left and I was hired by handling some of the more difficult cases, and he had spoken to her psychiatrist on several occasions. I ran back upstairs, fearful she might leave my office if left alone too long. When I walked in, Norma was sitting in a relaxed, composed manner.

"I'm sorry I upset you," she said in a conciliatory way. I breathed a sigh of relief, supposing I had overreacted.

"Well, I was worried about you Norma," I said.

"You bitch!" she screamed. It was like watching a kitten turn into a lion in a split second. "You knew what they were doing when they were fucking with . . . ." I did not wait to hear the end of her sentence. It was not a false alarm. I ran back to Paul's office as he hung up the telephone.

"The psychiatrist won't admit her," he said. "He thinks she is perfectly capable of making a rational decision as to whether she needs psychiatric help."

"He must be crazy himself. What do we do?" I asked, anxious for Paul to take the lead in this situation. This was not an incident I could take lightly and "learn from my mistakes." A mistake here could be dangerous.

"We'll have to call the police and hope they think she is potentially dangerous enough to bring her to the hospital. I'll call," he said.

"All right. I'll try to make sure she stays in one place," I said, running back upstairs.

She was not there. I ran up and down the hall looking in all the rooms. No Norma. I raced down the three flights of stairs and asked Laverne if she saw her.

"Sure," she said. "Norma just ran out of here like a bat out of hell."

"Do you know which direction she ran?" I asked.

"Sorry, babe. I didn't notice," she said, as she picked up the almost constantly ringing switchboard telephone.

I was back in Paul's office before he got the report to the police, and then we both ran to the street, searching for any sign of her. She was gone. I discussed the next course of action with my immediate supervisor, Maria, who was back from vacation, but she had been out of the building at the time of the incident. It was clear that Norma could not be allowed to stay at the shelter and that we had to ask her to leave, even if that meant she had nowhere to go. She presented too great a risk at this point, and our ethical responsibilities were to protect the group of women, rather than sacrifice their safety for the concerns of one person.

But there was a problem. I was scared—scared to tell Norma she could not stay at the shelter any longer. I knew she would return with the other women that night at 8 P.M., and I was afraid of what she might do when I told her she had to leave. I conjured up various scenarios: Norma pulling a knife from her purse and stabbing me as she had her employer, or attacking me with her bare hands, with all the force of her insanity. I knew such violence was unlikely, but I also knew it was not outside the realm of possibility.

I decided to call the local police precinct and explain my predicament. I gave the desk officer a rundown on the events of the afternoon, told him the woman was on parole for stabbing a man, and that I had to throw her out of the shelter that night. I asked if a police officer could come by around 8 P.M. to insure my safety and that of the other women. Oh how naive a beginner can be! The officer politely informed me that unless something violent was actually happening, an officer could not be sent.

"But why?" I asked, surprised at the refusal. I thought it was such a logical preventive course of action.

"Because there is too much going on in New York City. We can't tie up a car just in case something happens," he said.

Disappointed, I hung up. I pondered over the fact that getting my job meant I was supposed to know how to handle these things. So I told myself to handle it as best I could and hope for the best.

Dealing with emergencies is the type of thing you never really learn in school. The emotions, the physiological response, the immediacy—the experience teaches like nothing else. I reassured myself that everything would work out all right because it had to; then I tried to figure out the best way to tell her that she wouldn't be able to stay at the shelter.

I decided to use the main lobby area, which would allow me to isolate her from the other women, since no one was allowed in that part of the building. I asked one of the volunteers on duty that night to sit at the receptionist's desk, ready to call the police at the first sign of danger, while a new overnight aide, Gina, would stay in the shelter with the women. Bill, the maintenance man, was on duty in the building until midnight. He had a great sense of humor and was always ready to lend a hand if needed. I asked him to come to the lobby at 8 P.M. when the women arrived for dinner as a physical backup in case Norma tried something. He gladly complied.

It was a few minutes before eight, and I was anxious to get this ordeal over with. I was also very curious as to what mental state Norma would show up in, and wondered if there was any chance that she would not show up at all. I doubted that.

Eight P.M. Norma was in the group that came rushing through the door, each person eager to get her rest for the night after a long day in the summer sun. Norma seemed to be her affable self again, as she smiled and calmly agreed to come to the lobby with me to talk.

I pretended I was calm and confident. I had observed over the years that it often is not what people know or do but, unfortunately or not, how they present themselves that makes the greatest impression on people. I decided to act unflustered so Norma would not sense my nervousness . . . and then see if I fooled her.

We both sat on the lobby couch, with Mary, the volunteer, sitting behind us at the desk. "I'm sorry about what happened in the office today," I began, trying to be kind but firm. "Unfortunately, after that type of an outburst I can't let you stay at the shelter. I think it would be best if you looked for another place to stay."

"Yes, yes, I agree," Norma responded in a resigned tone. "I cannot stay in a place run by Mr. Paul. I was thinking anyway I really had to go."

"I'm glad you agree," I said, relieved beyond measure that it was going so smoothly.

"But there is the question of my money," Norma said. The agency's accounting department kept accounts for some of the shelter guests who got disability or public assistance checks. Norma had several hundred dollars in her account from disability payments that had accumulated during her period of hospitalization.

"I can have a check for your balance drawn up for you tomorrow, and you can come pick it up at the front desk," I said.

"Oh, that would be very kind," Norma smiled.

"Where do you think you will go?" I asked.

"I will go to a hotel. Do not worry about me. I will be fine."

I could not believe that she was being so agreeable. "We had better get your things," I said, deciding to try to keep conversation to a minimum. "I'll help you if you'd like." She would have to pick her things out from amongst the various articles in the communal lockers, and I wanted to be with her to ward off interaction with the other women.

We went up the steps to the backstage area where the lockers were kept. Norma removed clean linens from the linen locker and started going down the stairs. "Norma, there must be some mistake," I said. "I thought we both just agreed that it was best for you to leave the shelter."

"Yes, of course," she said, as her voice became injected with nervousness. "But not until I get my money."

"You'll get your money first thing in the morning, but I can't allow you to stay here tonight," I said.

"WHAT??!!" she exploded. Suddenly, the lion was snarling at me from the top step, as I looked at her from the four steps below. "Where will I go tonight with no money?"

"Maybe you know someone who will let you stay for the night. Maybe one of the drop-in centers. I don't know, and I'm sorry, but I cannot let you stay here," I said.

The furor of the afternoon had fully returned to her. It was not simple anger; it was an all-consuming rage that permeated Norma's entire body, setting it into a quivering, supercharged state that seemed to be feeding the psychotic thought patterns that had lately taken control of her. The electricity between us was ready to crackle and burst into flame. I tried to figure out what to do, as my eyes watched the transformation taking place in bloated seconds, Norma screaming and gesturing wildly.

"She's right," I thought. "It is cruel that I am throwing her out onto the street, but what kind of threat am I subjecting the other women to if I let her stay? Then again, she was quite tranquil a few seconds ago. I believe her when she says she knows she has to leave. If I press my point, she will surely do something, and I feel I am provoking her to madness. What if I tell her to go straight to bed and stay up and watch her?" It seemed the lesser of two evils.

"Okay. You can stay for tonight only," I said. "Calm down. I don't want to hurt you. I just have to do what is best for everybody. Tonight has to be the last night. You understand that, right?" I asked with outward composure while my insides were jumping around.

Norma nodded, her lips stretched tightly across a clenched jaw. The energy in her body seemed to drain, as the forward momentum of her stance relaxed into an upright pose. "Come, let's make your bed," I said, and Norma walked down the stairs. The women in the shelter had heard the screaming, and everyone seemed a little quieter, more guarded than usual.

After we made the bed, Norma immediately changed into her nightgown, got into bed, and fell asleep. It was as if her mental state had sapped every bit of energy from her exhausted body, finally allowing her to get some relief through sleep. I watched the shelter room with the overnight aide until midnight. Norma was in a deep sleep, and everything was quiet. Pat, the board president, and Mary, a very experienced volunteer, were on duty that night. Feeling secure that everything was under control and that I was leaving the shelter in capable hands, I left to spend the night at my girlfriend's apartment, just a few blocks away. As I went out the front door, I saw a police car parked in front of the shelter and learned that they had been there on and off all night. It was nice to know the department had responded to the extent that was possible.

The next morning, I had Norma's check drawn, and asked Laverne to tell me when she came for it. I met Norma downstairs. She was composed and peaceful. I had brought up a large carton with Norma's name scrawled on it from the laundry room, and asked her if she wanted to take any of the contents with her.

"Oh, I don't need any of that junk. Just give me my makeup

case, please," she said. I rummaged through the wrinkled articles of clothing and handed her the large, plastic pouch containing an array of cosmetics.

"Do you know where you are staying tonight?" I asked, feeling a sense of helplessness, worrying about her, worrying about who she might harm when in a psychotic state, knowing there was nothing I could do. It seemed so pathetic that this very sick woman was left to fend for herself. Perhaps her psychiatrist considered himself to be upholding her civil liberties by letting her decide for herself whether she needed more intensive treatment. But taken to this extreme, "upholding free will and determination" seemed to be an excuse for relinquishing society's duty to care for its most disabled members. But the law was with the psychiatrist.

If there were adequate community supports for mentally ill people, hospitalization would not be the only option and would not, in fact, be as necessary. However, there is a dearth of community psychiatric residences for the mentally ill, and with waiting lists years long at the few there are, hospitalization is often the only recourse for getting care. With few community supports for the mentally ill, further deterioration was to be expected. So conditions like Norma's flourish. There was no community residence for her, she could not be hospitalized, and now she could not even stay at the shelter. She was locked out of society, by society.

"I will stay in a hotel," Norma said. "I have several hundred dollars here. Do not concern yourself about me. I will not have trouble," she said resolutely.

We said goodbye, and she was off. I wondered for a moment how long that money would last. I knew the answer. In New York City, a few hundred dollars would pay for a seedy hotel room for a few weeks at most. Then what? I called Norma's parole officer and alerted her to what had transpired in the past two days so she could try to get her some help. I could think of nothing more to do.

I was relieved that the whole episode was over, but the sense of failure lingered on: failure to help this woman, failure I knew I shared with the whole of society. I could not change the system alone; solutions had to be worked on together.

I mulled over the events. Witnessing someone lose control is unnerving, perhaps because we all fear it could happen to us. When someone enters a private world, it evokes fear—fear of the unknown, fear of the irrational mind, fear of unprovoked violence. I had reacted strongly from fear of violence. I had overreacted in this situation, allowing my imagination to feed my fear. When I had decided to act unafraid, I became unafraid, for the most part. I was still highly charged, but not scared. People can sense whether you feel in control of a situation, as I was to learn many times over.

I was never scared after that. I tried to trust my instincts and believed that my concern for the other individual, coupled with a fearless attitude, would temper the other person enough to ward off any real threat. People often threaten to hurt others when *they* feel threatened. Sadly, a person with severe mental illness can feel imaginary threats all the time, and fear can become an everyday reality. The challenge was to pierce that reality, to form a bridge that says, "I am not a threat to you, and I want to ease your pain." It seemed to work.

In fact, there were fewer than a handful of potentially violent situations during my period of employment at the shelter. There were a few lesser incidents, when an inexperienced volunteer or graduate student helping out would feel there were threats all around. It simply took a little time to learn that most of the women were not dangerous. Many behaved in an unusual manner, and a few might have been potentially threatening, but most just needed the reassurance that they themselves were in a safe environment.

◆

I did not have time to mull over this episode. Ruminating was a luxury I could not afford. I had an interview scheduled for the program assistant job. The interviewee was recommended to me by a social worker in another program who knew that this woman was looking for a job working with homeless people.

Joan came into my office with a big smile and warm eyes. She was young, only twenty-two, energetic and committed. Joan had been living and working in a church-run program that ran a daily soup kitchen for the poor, most of whom were homeless. She had an easygoing personality, came with high recommendations, seemed like a responsible, solid type of person, and was genuinely interested in the position. I was thrilled and wanted to hire her on the spot. She seemed perfect. The procedure was that Maria second-interviewed those I thought were good for the job. I ran to her office and asked if she could interview Joan immediately. I did not want her to get away!

After their interview, Maria came to my office to discuss how it went. "She seems good. The only thing I'm worried about is that she may be a bit too idealistic. I've seen people like that burn out very quickly, but let's see how it goes. We can offer her $14,500 because she has directly related experience," she said.

I offered the job to Joan, who was waiting in Maria's office. She was happy, excited, and quickly accepted the offer. She would start in two weeks. I felt I had a fresh supply of oxygen. Joan was getting married on Labor Day weekend and requested two weeks off after that for her honeymoon, but she would be able to become familiar with the women during the two weeks before the wedding. I looked forward to having someone else to work with and to going home at an earlier hour for a few nights. Paul had been a support for me while Maria was on vacation, and now I could confer with Maria about problems, but for the most part I felt professionally isolated during the day and especially at night when the shelter was the only program in the building. It would be nice having another professional staffperson in the program to work with on a day-to-day basis.

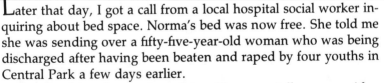

Later that day, I got a call from a local hospital social worker inquiring about bed space. Norma's bed was now free. She told me she was sending over a fifty-five-year-old woman who was being discharged after having been beaten and raped by four youths in Central Park a few days earlier.

Deirdre showed up an hour later. She was a tall woman with a medium frame, thin, wearing loosely hanging clothes that looked too big. She walked very slowly, dragging her right leg, which had been injured in the beating. Her face was swollen on one side to about twice its normal size and was varying shades of purple and blue. The eye on that side was open only slightly, pushed closed by the swollen flesh surrounding it. She was meek and polite, and the desperate urgency of most women who came in for a bed was absent. The spirit in this woman seemed gone altogether; she seemed indifferent to life.

I tried to be very gentle while going through the intake procedure. I expected her to be hysterical about what had happened in the park, imagining how traumatized I would be if I had been the victim. It became immediately apparent that Deirdre was handling the trauma by blocking it out as best she could. People have different ways of dealing with traumas and lesser problems: some people talk nonstop, feeling a need to communicate their pain to another human being; others close up and prefer not to talk about it at all, trying to face life stoically. Deirdre was definitely of the latter type, but something still seemed strange about her response to the attack. It was *too* controlled, *too* unemotional. It would be a long time before I would begin to have even a vague understanding of what she was about.

I asked Deirdre if she had spoken to anyone about the rape and told her there were self-help groups around, made up of other rape victims who shared their feelings and how they dealt with the attack. Deirdre raised an eyebrow and told me she had *not* been raped, just beaten. I was startled, as I had definitely been told otherwise. I did not want to push her, so I just apologized for my "mistake." She calmly told me that four teenagers had jumped her and beaten her while she slept in the park. I told her how sorry I was and that I imagined it must have been a frightening and painful experience for her. She just shrugged.

I had established an informal policy that every new woman had to have a case plan, a plan worked out by the woman and myself that outlined in very basic form what steps were necessary in order to resume independent living, such as get medical attention, file for disability benefits, apply for housing, and so on. It was a beginning sketch that let the woman know we expected her to be willing to take steps to function on her own again, and that we accepted the responsibility to help her take those steps, when necessary. Creating such a plan with Deirdre was not possible at this time. We got as far as getting some background information.

She told me in her quiet, matter-of-fact, and well-spoken way that although she was born in Belgium, she had grown up in New York City. She moved to Italy when she was forty, living there for eight years before running out of money. She moved back to New York City, applied for public assistance, and lived in an apartment for several years until her public assistance was cut off during the first wave of massive, federally initiated cutbacks. Deirdre applied for a fair hearing and won, but was cut off again within the year. She then got an eviction notice because she could not pay her rent. Deciding never to "get involved with the government again," Deirdre gave up and moved into Central Park, where she had been living for the past two years. She had a brief stint in a shelter, but was thrown out because she refused to apply for benefits and would do nothing to help herself become independent. She seemed to be making an effort to be polite, but it was obviously an effort for her to speak.

I tried to fill in the missing pieces. She seemed to be well educated, judging by the way she spoke, yet she said she had never worked. She might have come from a family with a little money, which she lived on until it ran out. She said she had no living family members and had never married. I suspected a mental breakdown somewhere along the way, although I was only guessing.

Deirdre was someone for whom it was difficult to determine if she became mentally ill before or after becoming homeless. Some people had breakdowns before; some people became mentally ill because of the incredible strain of living on the streets or in shelters. The two groups were often indistinguishable, because by the time they came for or were cajoled into getting help, they were too sick to give a clear picture of the events that brought them to their current position. Besides, revealing a psychiatric history was not the most pleasant thing to do: there was the fear of being sent back to the hospital, there was embarrassment. In our society, we have not gotten to the point where mental illness is seen as a true sickness; it is still perceived as the individual's own fault. If one has diabetes, one is sick. If one is paranoid, one is frightening, weak, to blame—a perception that helps us imagine we can protect ourselves from a similar fate. So those suffering from mental illness were often afraid to admit it: afraid to admit it to themselves, afraid to admit it to others, alone with a problem medical science has not yet found a cure for.

Deirdre's thought patterns were confused. It took me over an hour to get what little information I did. She was having a very hard time remembering any particulars.

"Where was your last apartment?" I asked.

"Oh, I don't know. Downtown somewhere."

"How did you pay for it?"

"It was paid for by the government so I won't ever go back again. The government is corrupt and they are trying to kill people."

"What do you mean it was paid for by the government?"

"I would get a check every month and pay my landlord with it."

"What was the check for?"

"I don't know what you mean."

"Was it a disability check from Social Security? Or a public assistance check? An unemployment check?"

"I don't know. Public assistance, I think."

On and on, trying to piece the fragments of her life together. Then the case plan came.

"Deirdre, I know you have just been through a lot, so we don't have to do this now," I said. "But everyone who is given a bed has to work out a plan with me to get her on her own again."

"I don't want anything. I just want a bed," she said blankly.

"You'll get the bed," I said. "Don't worry about that. But after you have had a few days to rest, we should talk about how we can work towards finding you a permanent living situation."

"All I want is a bed," she repeated. "If I have to do anything else I won't stay. I just want to be left alone."

"Where would you go?" I asked.

"Back to the park," she said evenly.

It made me shudder. How horribly pitiful this was. "I don't want you to do that. Why don't you plan on staying for a month and think it over, and we'll talk again at the end of August," I offered.

"Okay," she said, "but I won't change my mind. Thank you."

I feared she would not change her mind. What would I do then? Just let her stay, doing nothing for herself indefinitely? The argument for setting limits and case plans was to help us serve the women, not do them a disservice by only giving them temporary shelter, which in some cases made it easier and more tempting for a woman to turn off to life, to slide into an existence requiring as little personal responsibility as possible, to become severely depressed. But in Deirdre's case, she had already turned off to life; she seemed incapable of handling responsibility for her own life.

Some might argue she was taking the ultimate responsibility: surviving with absolutely no money, pitted against nature and society in the heart of New York City on her own terms. But from my perspective, she was presently incapable of making rational decisions for herself, and that necessarily altered her ability to handle that responsibility, altering what was reasonable to expect from her as well. I resolved that the best we might ever do for her was to provide shelter, wondering if the psychological wounds of the attack would ever heal, wondering what horrors she might have suffered before. We would have to take it very slow with Deirdre.

That night I introduced her to some of the other women and showed her the available bed. It was against the far wall, closest to the entrance door. This made it a little more private than the others since it had only one bed next to it. It was therefore coveted by the women. I was glad it happened to be the free bed, because Deirdre was clearly nervous to be around so many people in such close proximity.

I left her, to deal with Jackie, who was complaining that they did not get good snacks anymore. Michelle joined in. She was a very austere-looking woman with large, horn-rimmed glasses, her hair in a tidy bun, and conservative, neat clothes. Jackie wanted Oreos; Michelle wanted pâté. The workers before me had apparently bought a variety of cookies every night, which made Jackie happy, and supplied Michelle with enough pâté to sustain her every day. When I began the job, I discontinued these practices. Cookies had little nutritional value and were expensive, but since the women were used to them, I compromised by buying fruit-bar cookies and more fresh fruit.

As for the pâté, it was outrageously expensive, and I could not see catering to a woman's taste for daily pâté as her main food source. Giving one person such preferential treatment without good reason did not make sense to me. Michelle claimed she had a delicate system and could only eat pâté. I thought that might be possible, but thought it was reasonable to ask her to explore other options. I asked her to talk to our health team about diet and her system, and then to tell me what she could and could not eat. She refused. I did not buy pâté.

Michelle was getting unemployment checks, and I observed that she never bought pâté out of this money. She ate the shelter food for dinner every night, and, judging by her appetite, she was not suffering from the experience. But she never passed an opportunity to glare at me. She loved that pâté.

While I was once again explaining why I had stopped the cookies and pâté, I had not noticed that Deirdre was dragging large blackboards on wheels across the room. When I turned around, the women closest to her bed were already complaining.

"Why should she get to block off her bed? I want to do that, too," Kathy said.

Deirdre had blockaded her bed by sliding a large blackboard to each side, except for the head, which was against the wall. I walked over and explained to Deirdre and the others that I could not allow that type of blockade because of fire regulations. Deirdre argued with me, a sharp edge in her voice that I had not heard before, but finally stopped when she realized it was not debatable.

"Well, I don't know if I can stay," she said. "I thought I'd have more privacy. I didn't know everyone wanted to watch me naked."

With patience that was growing patchy, I assured her that no one wanted to look at her body, and suggested we get a nightgown from the donation closet. She declined the offer, got in bed between the sheets, wriggled out of her clothes, and then went to the snack table for coffee with the sheet wrapped around her like a sari.

No one noticed.

Chapter 4

⌐Is There a Doctor in⌐ the House?

◆

⌐The shelter operation was gradually becoming more organized. The laundry room, the only area that had not had an overhaul, was scheduled for a face-lift on a humid summer evening. Richard, a young community minister, was the volunteer on duty for the early part of the evening, and I knew I could count on him to help. During the week, I had asked the women to put all of their belongings in marked bags, or in the new cartons I had left in the room, so that we would not inadvertently sort through their belongings.

Richard and I sorted through the unmarked bags strewn about the room, putting aside any valuables before throwing out most of the bug-ridden contents. It was a dirty job, and the heat of the summer night made it all the more distasteful. Bags of crumpled tissues, bits of food, dirty combs, magazines, photographs of loved ones, unpaired shoes, makeup, and clothes, clothes, and more clothes. The "valuables" consisted of some usable umbrellas and about twenty-five cents worth of change.

The donation closet was next on our list. Much of the clothing in the closet was dirty and torn, and I wondered if the people who donated those things really thought they were doing anybody a favor by giving away what should have been thrown in the garbage. We salvaged what we could and threw the rest of it in its rightful place. Much of the space in the other closet and cabinets was filled with bags belonging to women who had long since gone but whose names I recognized from the file folders in my office. We tossed almost everything. If the women had not been back in six months or more, I doubted they would return for the things, and we simply did not have the room to save them. The room looked one hundred percent better when we were through, the air smelled a little less stale, and a dozen heavy-duty garbage bags stuffed with discarded articles lined the hall.

We came upstairs to the shelter and collapsed in the snack room chairs. Gina had been supervising, as usual.

"Aaagh! You filthy pigs! This is a shithole for pigs!"

The screams came from the backstage area. I recognized Nancy's voice as I ran across the auditorium to the dimly lit stage steps. My insides felt momentarily suspended in icy fear when I saw Nancy lying on her back in a pool of blood, her feet on the top step of the stairs and her head on the landing, four steps below. She was crying in big, gulping sobs and shouting with each new breath.

"This is pig heaven! You're running a filthy shithole for pigs," she screamed.

"Nancy, don't move. We'll get you help," I said. "Call an ambulance," I told Jane, the nighttime volunteer who had come in a few minutes earlier. Gina ran to get cold towels.

Nancy, seventy years old, overweight, and bleeding from her head and right hand, was trying to get up.

"Try not to move. You may have broken something. The ambulance should be here soon," I said, remembering from first aid class that you are never supposed to move someone who has fallen because if something is broken, improper movement can cause further damage.

Gina came with cold, wet towels, which we gently applied to Nancy's head. It was not bleeding too heavily, appearing to be a bad cut but not a serious one. Her hand was another story. I struggled to overcome the urge to throw up as we put another towel to her bleeding fingers. Her forefinger and middle finger were bleeding profusely; the skin of both was hanging in strips, as if someone had sliced them in half to expose the internal flesh.

Jane returned. "I can't get through. The telephone's not working."

I had called the phone company many times because the shelter extension often went dead, but they never seemed able to correct this recurring problem. I ran into the main lobby and called 911 from the switchboard. "Please send an ambulance immediately. A seventy-year-old woman fell down several steps in our shelter. She landed on her back, cut her head, and her fingers are ripped open," I told them. I then asked Alice, one of the shelter guests, to stand at the front door and wave down the ambulance to make sure they came directly to the shelter entrance. Meanwhile, Nancy continued to howl in her gravelly voice while struggling to get up.

"Nancy, wait just a few more minutes," I implored.

"I'm not lying here another second. Someone's trying to kill me!" she shrieked. "This is a pighole, I tell you!"

"Calm down," I said. "No one is trying to kill you."

"Yes, yes they are," she said earnestly. "I was standing on top of the steps and then it got all black and the ghosts came and pushed me over."

Nancy was mentally healthy, although easily confused, but now and then she spoke of demons as matter-of-factly as of what she had for dinner. She was wriggling around, trying to get her feet on level ground. I was afraid that if I did not help her get up, she would hurt herself more by insisting on doing it alone. I eased the upper part of her body up and back while Gina eased her feet down and wiped up the pools of blood. With one of us on each side, we walked Nancy to the door and sat her in a chair to wait for the ambulance, which came within minutes. They began wrapping her hand, and warned me that moving someone after a fall could be dangerous and not to do it again.

Alice said she wanted to go with Nancy to the hospital to give her moral support. Alice, a forty-year-old recovering alcoholic, had taken Nancy under her wing since arriving at the shelter about a year ago. Nancy was unsteady on her feet and often needed help with bathing and other daily living skills. She had an engaging personality, and Alice and she had become friends, Alice lending a hand whenever she could. Nancy trusted Alice, so we hoped she would be a reassuring presence for her in the hospital. They were off within minutes.

Everyone began settling down for the night. I stayed until 11:15 P.M. when the lights were turned off, gradually unwinding and letting the tension of the evening drain from my body. I was thankful that a girlfriend of mine had offered her parents' apartment to me for the night. They were out of town, and she thought I would enjoy not commuting to Long Island for a night. I took a cab to the apartment, some twenty blocks away, leaving my phone number with Gina before leaving.

The apartment was air conditioned, modern, with a balcony overlooking the jewel-like city skyline. I was in heaven. I had just sunk into the couch when the phone rang. It was a hospital nurse, who had gotten my number from Gina. Nancy had been taken to the emergency room about three hours earlier, so I expected to be getting a progress report.

"This is the head nurse in the emergency room," she said.

"Yes," I said anxiously. "How is Nancy?"

"We haven't examined her yet," she said. "She's crawling with head and body lice. The doctors won't touch her."

"What?!" I asked, with incredulity. "What do you mean, they won't touch her?"

"Well, we stitched her hand, but because of the lice, we can't examine her to determine why she blacked out before falling. Nobody will touch her. Can she be sent back to the shelter?" she asked.

"You've got to be kidding me! No, she cannot come back. This is incredible," I said, my blood pressure rising as I fought to control my anger. "You've got to examine her. She's in the hospital and you're responsible for treating her. Why doesn't someone wash the lice off? You can't just leave her there."

"Well, I'll see what I can do," she said.

After calling Gina to tell her what had transpired, I paced the room to work off my anger. A hospital that does not want to treat someone because of lice? I could not believe it, yet I had just heard it firsthand. I wondered how homeless people managed in a society that was so squeamish. Those doctors must have seen worse than lice. Did a lice-ridden person seem less worthy of good health and treatment than a squeaky-clean human being?

I tried to push these thoughts out of my mind for a moment to focus on the more immediate problem. How did Nancy get lice? She bathed every few days and appeared to be clean. The "rule" in the shelter was daily bathing, but it was an elastic rule, like most of the others. Nancy liked being clean, but daily showering was a bit much because it required a great deal of physical exertion for her to go down the basement stairs to the shower area. The cleansing she did at the sink in the main floor bathroom, in between showering, had apparently not been thorough enough.

"If she has lice, Louise must have them for sure," I thought, thinking of the little woman who never bathed, to my knowledge. We would have to have everyone examined. Lice spread easily, either by physical contact with the infected person or by touching or rubbing against the infected person's clothing or bedding. This was the first time I was dealing with lice on a level more intimate than that between a textbook and reader.

I began to squirm a little. I had been touching Nancy after the fall, putting my arms around her to help lift and support her while walking. "Oh no," I thought. "That would be miserable if this one night that I happen to be at the Gorman's I have lice and get it on their furniture." (Lice can get embedded in the upholstery.) I threw my clothes in their washing machine, aware that lice do not always die in a normal washing and that you're supposed to burn infested clothing. I was not in the mood to figure out how to burn my clothes safely in their apartment, so I figured I would take my chances with the washing machine. I took a steaming hot shower and scrubbed myself ferociously many times over. Feeling reassured, I read a little and dozed off, only to wake up to a 3:30 A.M. phone call from the hospital.

"She's all cleaned up, and we're admitting her for tests," the nurse said. "It looks like she may have some heart trouble, which could have caused the blackout."

"Okay, I'll call the hospital tomorrow to follow up," I said. "Thanks for seeing she got cared for," I said, still angry that I had to argue with the nurse earlier before she saw that care was provided for Nancy.

I wondered if we might be able to make more headway with Nancy now, about moving to a nursing home. She could not go on living the way she was for much longer. She was no longer capable of caring for herself in an apartment and was too mistrustful to consider home care, even if we could find an affordable apartment (finding an affordable apartment in New York City for a frail old lady on Social Security was like trying to find the whitest hair on her head). I was afraid if we did not move quickly, Nancy would not last once the cold weather hit, with its slippery, icy sidewalks. Nancy needed help fast if she was to survive the winter. It was depressing to think about it all for too long. I went to sleep.

◆

The following day I went to Diane, the settlement house nurse, and asked for her advice regarding the lice.

"Well, I can examine everyone for head lice tonight," she said. "Only everyone has to comply or else it will be a waste of time. If I don't examine everyone, someone may still have the lice, or lice eggs, and they can start spreading."

"No problem," I said. "Come at 8 P.M. and I'll explain the problem to everyone and why everyone has to be examined. This is a potential health hazard and we can't take any chances."

That evening I told the shelter guests that lice had been found, explained how they spread, how they laid many eggs that could hatch later, and so forth. Everyone was quite willing to be examined except Louise and Jean. Louise simply did not want anyone to touch her. She was a sixty-two-year-old, tiny 4'10" woman, who most typically embodied the "bag woman" image that many people had of women without homes (the image is actually quite atypical of the majority of homeless women). Louise never bathed at the shelter despite active encouragement to do so, yet looked more bedraggled than dirty.

One of the first shelter guests, Louise was originally found sitting on the neighborhood streets encrusted with urine and filth. She had lived on the sidewalks for a long time, was very withdrawn, and only came into the shelter after much effort by the former staff members. I had decided it would be counterproductive to throw her out for not bathing when she had come relatively far. I hoped that she would eventually shed some of the layers of clothing she wore and take regular showers, but I realized at the same time that she might not, and that providing shelter on compromised terms might be the best we could ever do for her.

I had not been able to reach Louise at all. Inquiries about her life, or suggestions about long-term planning were met with trigger-quick responses: "Get the fuck away from me! Come back to me when you're married with children. I don't have to talk to you."

Yet talk about the weather or *my* life, and she was cordial and warm, shy, with a smile that seemed especially beautiful because it was an instant transformation from the usual grim countenance hidden beneath the big, knit cap pulled past her eyebrows. The only clue to her past that I ever got from her was that she once had a child, or children, that died. Who was she thirty years ago? A young mother? Someone's lover? Someone's child. What happened along the way that led her to live on the streets? Was there anyone in the world who cared if she lived or died? Perhaps the time she spent living on the sidewalks left her so numb that she did not realize there could be more, that it could be better. Questions. Theories. Guesses. I had lice to deal with.

"Louise, everyone has to be examined. Lice are contagious. All Diane has to do is look at your scalp and hair," I said.

I was talking to a sheet. Louise had jumped into her bed with all her clothes on, including her shoes, and pulled the outer sheet completely over her head. Her nose and wire-rimmed glasses made little peaks in the sheet.

"Go fuck yourself," she muttered.

I'm talking to a sheet that curses at me, I thought. What a unique job this is!

"No one is going to hurt you. Just take the sheet off your head and Diane can examine you right here," I entreated.

"Get a husband. Then I'll talk to you," she responded.

This went on for several minutes, after which she acquiesced to an examination in bed. Much to my amazement, Diane found nothing and said her scalp and hair (rarely seen under the hat, even on ninety-degree days) were clean. "She must be washing it somewhere," Diane said. This was good news. I wondered where she washed and whether she just needed more prodding to change her clothes on a regular basis. The many layers usually remained on her body throughout the night. I thanked Louise for complying and sought Jean.

"It is absurd. You know we are clean. It is the others who are dirty," Jean snapped.

"I know you're incredibly clean, but lice are contagious. You could have gotten some by touching someone's sheets or clothing. It doesn't mean you're not clean," I said.

"I absolutely refuse," she said, clamping her jaw in a steely grip.

I got an unwelcome impression that she was not going to budge. Tough as Louise was, I had known I could eventually soften her; Jean was another story. One could sense a stubborn will and absoluteness about her when she made up her mind on a subject.

I spoke to Diane in private, questioning whether we should bend the rule for her, considering her personal hygiene standards. "If you make an exception for her and her mother," Diane replied, "you run the risk of having lice or lice eggs in the shelter and putting everyone else in jeopardy. It doesn't matter how clean she is. There's always the chance the lice or eggs were transmitted, what with the close quarters everyone's living in."

"Okay, okay," I said. "I hate to do it, but I think I'll have to give her an ultimatum."

I went back to Jean, with Lily smiling innocently and uncomprehendingly by her side. "Jean, there really can be no debating this issue. Diane says it is too great a risk. You and your mother must be examined," I said.

"I refuse. It is a joke having someone check my hair. We won't do it," she replied hotly.

"I hate to do this," I said, "but I will have to give you a choice. Either go through with the two-minute examination or you cannot stay here."

"Then we will leave," she said curtly, hustling Lily toward their beds and belongings. I followed.

"Be reasonable," I urged. "Your mother is eighty-four years old. Where will you go? Ask Lily what *she* wants to do."

Jean spoke quickly in Polish to Lily, who replied sharply to her in their native tongue.

"She will do it. I will not," she said coldly. "I'll sleep outside and come in in the morning to help my mother get dressed."

"Well, I wish you'd change your mind, but if that's your choice, I guess there's nothing more I can say," I said, feeling horrible but helpless, feeling I had to do what I did.

Diane had completed the examinations. No one had active lice, but lice eggs were found in Kathy's hair. We gave her special shampoo and a small-toothed lice comb. I got ready to head towards Penn Station, hoping I would not have to deal with lice again for a long time. Leslie was cursing out an imaginary communist, Danny the cat was snoring, and Jean was sitting on the outdoor steps. Another night's end, for me anyway.

The next day, to my relief, Jean agreed to have the examination and was found to be clean.

◆

Health-related problems reigned for several weeks, a phenomenon I would become used to. Kathy, who had expressed such hope about getting out of the shelter on my first night on the job, now came into my office to tell me she had an ulcerated leg. Her tone had become apathetic, her expectations dwarfed, her hope diminished.

During my first week of work, Kathy had come into my office to ask for help in getting out of the shelter. Like so many of the other women, she thought I had inside information on housing. Like the others, she was disappointed to learn that I did not, disappointed to learn that their inability to find low-cost housing was not a reflection of their house-hunting skills but a reflection of society's housing priorities. The low-cost housing stock had shrunk, and those squeezed out would have to suffer. My own inability to produce new housing possibilities scraped away more layers of disbelief about their situation. There simply was no available low-cost housing.

Kathy had lived in Queens for most of her life. Married and divorced, she had moved in with her widowed mother and worked as a secretary. Several years later, Kathy's mother died in a car accident. Kathy's salary was not enough to meet the monthly household payments without the addition of her mother's Social Security checks. She struggled to find a way to manage, eventually suffered from a nervous breakdown, lost the home, and found herself homeless.

Two and a half years, a brief hospitalization, and two shelters later, Kathy urgently wanted to find a permanent place to live, and she hoped to work again when her living situation became more stabilized. The monthly Social Security checks she received for mental disability would be discontinued when she resumed employment. Other than finding an affordable apartment, there had been no impediments in Kathy's way in order to live on her own again: she was physically healthy, responsible, had regained her mental health, and had a source of income until she found work. Kathy had already tried all the avenues I knew of for possible housing. I cringed as the weeks flew by, wondering how long Kathy could ward off the deleterious effects of living in a shelter. Not long enough—Kathy lifted her pant leg to reveal a ballooned calf, covered with open, red, oozing sores.

"That's awful!" I gasped. "Have you shown this to the health team?"

"Yes," she said, "that's why I'm talking to you about it. They've been giving me ointment, but it's not working. I need to be off my feet for the swelling to go down."

"How did you get these ulcers?" I asked, incredulous at the severity of the swelling and the breadth of the sores.

"I retain water, and with the summer heat and nowhere to rest in the daytime, my legs swell more, until the skin breaks open. There's nowhere to sit during the day without being told to move along after a while," she said.

I had observed this fact on many occasions, but I had never thought about the implications it had for a homeless person. One could walk for blocks and blocks without seeing a bench. Sidewalks, buildings, cars, but nowhere to sit down; everyone practically runs. Central Park might have served as a haven, were it not for the violence recently perpetrated on the vulnerable taking refuge there. Deirdre's ordeal, the murder of a homeless woman weeks before in the park, and the media's full coverage of both had served as a powerful deterrent to resting on the plentiful benches found amidst the greenery.

Kathy and I worked out a plan for her to stay at a local YMCA for two weeks, the time period the health team deemed necessary for the swelling to subside. At twenty-five dollars a night, the Y was the cheapest available living space. Kathy would pay as much as she could with her disability check, and the settlement house agency would pay for the rest out of the emergency relief budget line. Kathy was relieved, although she had displayed a lack of alarm over the situation that I found disconcerting. She had crossed the line between urgency and acceptance, anger and apathy.

It disgusted me to see her sores, imagining the pain and discomfort. Teenage memories flashed through my mind as I remembered noticing homeless people for the first time, meandering about Penn Station, their legs caked with blood and pus from ulcerated sores. At the time, I had conjectured that it was a disease one got from alcoholism. Here I was, many years later, learning the simple truth that these ugly wounds could result from not having a place to sit.

◆

For Kathy, that would soon change, as the day program was scheduled to open in a month. Joan was working the 3 to 11 P.M. shift at the shelter during the two weeks prior to her wedding; she would assume primary responsibility for the day program when it opened in September, shifting to a regular 9 to 5 day at that time. Joan's background and personality seemed well suited to the challenge. A local church was donating their basement for program use, space that had been used for a few months during the previous winter as a place for the women to come in out of the cold. We wanted it to become more than a daytime shelter; it would be a place where women could avail themselves of services and resources helpful in building independence, a place to find some enjoyment to cut into the stretch of days with no place to call home, a place where women who were ready to move out of the shelter, but still lacked an affordable apartment could wait. We decided to develop groups, with the help of volunteers, concerning housing, health, jobs, and any other relevant topics. Social and cultural groups would be formed as well, to promote stimulation and interaction, to combat the depression that stalked the long hours.

The dinner program would also be reinstituted in September, with dinner at a different church each night except for Saturday and Sunday, which would still be at the shelter. The volunteer coordinators for each site were contacted and all were set to go. Another staffperson would be hired to work the 3 to 11 P.M. shift Monday through Friday and would be responsibile for covering each dinner site and making sure everything at the shelter was in order before clocking out. Slowly, slowly, a sense of organization grew out of the chaos and a means of staving off the effects of living in a state of upheaval and helping those in need build their lives again began to look possible.

———————————————◆———————————————

At least one woman had rebuilt her life already, with minimal support from the shelter—Alice. Alice had spent the last year at the shelter working on overcoming her addiction to alcohol, attending an intensive day-treatment program for alcoholics run at a local hospital, as well as Alcoholics Anonymous meetings. Alice's hospital social worker was trying to get her a room at a newly opened residence for recovering alcoholics. The day-treatment program was running the residence, renting out rooms to people in their program who could benefit from living in a supportive setting.

Alice was a well-educated, bright woman of Scottish descent. She had applied to a local university that ran a counselor-training program for recovering alcoholics and was eager to enter this program and eventually be able to help other addicts overcome their addiction. Alice was as helpful as most volunteers, keeping supplies organized, making a large urn of coffee each night, helping some of the older women navigate the washrooms, and doing other small kindnesses. She often sat in the lounge for hours, talking with a volunteer or two, forming friendships.

Unknown to me, June, a conscientious volunteer who came every Thursday night, offered her family's apartment to Alice for two weeks while they were on vacation. She thought it would be a nice break from shelter life for Alice. She could not imagine that any harm could come from such an arrangement since Alice seemed so responsible. What June did not realize was that alcoholism is a gripping disease, capable of transforming an individual with just one drink.

When Alice did not show up at the shelter, I asked Kathy, who was friendly with her, if she knew where she was. Kathy told me of the arrangement, conjecturing that Alice probably thought June had filled me in on the plan. I was quite surprised about the arrangement, and worried about Alice. Instant independence could be dangerous if there were no plans to protect the vulnerable points. I rang June's phone, but got no answer.

True to my fears, Alice showed up two night later, drunk. Gina said she came in with a man, looked around the laundry room somewhat frantically for her belongings, and then came upstairs, yelling incoherently and telling everyone she would get them all out soon. Gina had to usher her to the door. My heart sank as I thought of how far she had journeyed toward recovery, wondering if she was now back to ground zero.

Later in the week, Alice dropped by my office. She was scared. June had left a well-stocked liquor cabinet in the apartment, and Alice discovered she could not resist the temptation to sample it. She wanted to be in control of her addiction, had thought she was, and was embarrassed and frightened by the transgression.

Alice spent only a week or two more at the shelter. Her room at the residence came through, and she left the shelter armed with a new awareness of the enemy alcohol's strength and of the need for her to have ready a constant line of defense. With a promise to visit the shelter as a volunteer, Alice left to start her new life. She remained true to her promise, and to my knowledge, hers remains a happy ending.

Alcohol was a foe we had to deal with only a handful of times, occasionally having to ask an addict to leave the shelter permanently for refusing to accept help. In total, there were about four alcoholics who had been to the shelter over the course of eighteen months. The only drug addict at the shelter during that period of time was Stacie, a former heroin addict and a witty, caring person who was proud of her Jewish heritage.

Stacie had several drug-related crises during my first few months at the shelter. She was in a methadone maintenance program where methadone, a controllable drug, was dispensed to heroin addicts every day at a local clinic. The theory is that methadone satisfies the addict's needs while not grossly altering his or her mental state, and because of its controllability, the level administered can be reduced over a period of time. In ideal cases, the level of methadone is gradually reduced until it is no longer needed at all. In addition to the methadone Stacie got at the clinic, she would take any other drugs she could get her hands on. She loved being high, despite the fact that she often came down with a crash.

An outreach program had arranged Stacie's visits to the clinic, did intensive supportive counseling with her, helped manage her finances, and put her on the list for a new residence for homeless people that the organization was going to operate. Stacie's outreach worker, Elaine, was great. She put her heart and soul into helping Stacie develop a more stable lifestyle, and Elaine's belief in her seemed to help Stacie herself believe in her own capabilities and self-worth.

It had been agreed between Stacie, Elaine, and myself that we would give Stacie six dollars from her account each morning, the daily allotment her monthly public assistance (welfare) checks afforded her. Six dollars a day barely paid for the bare necessities; two dollars for bus fare to and from the clinic left her with four dollars for lunch and any other needs. Stacie knew that if she handled her own finances she would spend her monthly check in one day just on drugs. Stacie was fifty-five and had been an addict for thirty to forty years. There was little likelihood that her body could sustain continued abuse, and she knew it.

Nevertheless, twice that summer Stacie had to be taken to the emergency room, both times for overdosing on Elevil, a prescription drug that when taken in excess will produce a high. Much to my amazement (God only knows why I had any shred of naiveté intact), I found out Stacie was getting the Elevil from a doctor, who gave the pills to her in exchange for monies he illegally collected from using her Medicaid card. Stacie naturally protected his identity.

The first time I witnessed Stacie on an Elevil high was on a hot night, around 8 P.M., when the women came in for dinner. Staggering, eyes glazed and half shut, slurring words and semi-sentences, and falling asleep while still standing, Stacie was not aware of her surroundings. I decided to take her to the emergency room, only two blocks away, not wanting to take any chances, since I suspected a mixture of drugs could aggravate Stacie's heart ailments. We walked the two short blocks, Stacie leaning on me for support and groggily asking me where we were every few steps.

When we arrived at the emergency room, I realized help was not necessarily at hand. The nurse on duty was abrupt, and her attitude suggested that she would rather not have to bother with homeless people. I bristled at her display of disgust, wondering what daily encounters with people who act repulsed must do to one's sense of pride and self-image. If enough outsiders treat a per-

son as if he or she is a scrap of refuse, unworthy of respect, that
person may eventually begin to believe and internalize the percep-
tions. That person may forget, like his or her critics, that we are inherently each as worthy as every other human being.

We sat in the plastic scoop chairs, Stacie dozing off, waking and
muttering, dozing, waking, muttering. Ambulances carrying
bleeders, chokers, heart failure victims. In and out, the machine
churned on. From time to time, I would ask why Stacie was not
seen yet. The answer was always the same: more pressing emergencies to handle. At about 11 P.M., Paul showed up. He had seen
us leaving the shelter and was concerned when we had not
returned. After explaining that we were still waiting to be seen, he
generously suggested I leave, offering to stay with Stacie himself.
I was exhausted, and thankful to get relief. Stacie, who needed relief much more, had to continue waiting.

The following morning I found out that Stacie was finally seen
at 5 A.M. Paul practically had to tie her down to get her to stay there
after all those long, uncomfortable hours. She was admitted and
treated for several days.

The experience was not enough to scare her from overdosing
again. With drugs exerting such a powerful force on Stacie's body,
it was a constant uphill battle to control the addiction, made worse
by her environment. With no place to go and no structure to her
days, Stacie was daily prey to the drug pushers who roamed the
streets with their temptations. The stress of being without a home
made her more vulnerable to depression. To relieve the depression, she craved getting high, and if there was any way to procure
drugs, short of stealing, she did it. Then she suffered all the more.

Joan slept at the shelter one night during her first week of work
and witnessed the physical manifestations of Stacie's sprees. Stacie
had a minor seizure very early in the morning. The aide saw the
seizure and woke Joan, who got to Stacie's bed in time to see her
body being thrown about by a large seizure. The police were called
(they dispatch the ambulance), and when the paramedics arrived
shortly afterwards, Stacie's heart had stopped. The paramedics
worked on and revived her while the other women looked on in
silent fear, life and death commingling in the air. She was hospitalized for several weeks this time.

We allowed Stacie to stay at the shelter, even though she was
still involved with drugs, for one reason—there was hope. Stacie

was involved in the methadone rehabilitation program, and she was *trying* to stay away from drugs. With her history of years of drug abuse, it was unrealistic to expect her never to transgress. We are human; we fail. But the will to overcome was in her. She *wanted* a decent life. That single factor gave her the chance to achieve it. She *wanted* it.

Will, the desire to seize life, was a quality that could not be underestimated. Some people were so beaten that their will seemed to have vanished. Their spirits were broken; they had given up. I found that a broken spirit could be the most devastating crippler of all.

One August afternoon, the embodiment of a broken spirit walked into my office. The woman had such a look of blank resignation on her face that it was surprising she was able to muster the motivation to move her limbs.

"I'm, Margaret, Jackie's mother. I want to stay at the shelter," she said, as she lowered her heavy body mechanically into a chair.

I was shocked, having read Margaret's file. She and Jackie had come to the shelter together over a year ago. Margaret was diagnosed as schizophrenic, had periods of hysteria, and had been in the habit of calling the police at odd times of the night to scream obscenities into the phone. *This* was the docile woman with the potatolike countenance I was looking at? Jackie had eventually been instrumental in convincing Margaret to go to a long-term state hospital for the mentally ill (anything over six weeks is considered long-term). According to the files, Margaret would have been in about three months now.

"Weren't you in the hospital, Margaret?" I asked. "Did they discharge you with no place to go?"

"They told me to go back to my apartment, but I can't go because there's no furniture and the electricity doesn't work," she said, speaking in quick, monotone syllables.

I had read in the file that Margaret and Jackie had an apartment in Brooklyn they still paid rent on, but it had not been clear from the notes why they did not return. After a fairly lengthy conversa-

tion with Margaret, and a phone conversation with her hospital social worker, I told Margaret she could stay for a three-week period
only, during which time I would work on making the apartment
habitable. Reluctantly, she agreed. It was to be the beginning of
one of the most complicated entanglements I would ever be involved in.

That night, the other women saw Margaret at dinner. An electric
current of shock zipped around the room. Several women asked
me what happened to her, conjecturing that the drugs at the hospital had turned her into this slowly shuffling zombie. I had never
met her before, yet I had to silently agree with the women that the
half-crazed, angry woman I imagined her to have been might have
been more welcome, less eerie than this shell that appeared to have
heart and soul cut out.

Heart and soul were still there. To carve through the layers of
numbness to reach them would take time.

Nancy also returned from the hospital that week. She was supposed to rewrap the bandages on her fingers and apply medication
to the wounds four times a day. For Nancy, these requisites to
proper healing were not easily met. It was difficult for her to
manipulate the bandages with one hand, she had nowhere to wash
her fingers when she took the old bandage off, and it was hard for
her to remember to do it in the first place.

I tried to help Nancy whenever she remembered to stop into my
office. I never would have been a good nurse. The first time we unwrapped those fingers, I had to squelch the urge to wince and pull
away. Black stitches were zigzagged up, down, and across her
fingers, holding together purple, swollen flesh that oozed. The
healing process would be slow. She still refused to consider nursing home placement, although the medical form that had to be included with any nursing home application was filled out during
her hospitalization, just in case. If she reconsidered, at least we
would have completed one step in the process. In the meantime,
we wrapped and unwrapped her bandages, helped her in the
shower, helped shampoo and comb her hair, and hoped she would
survive.

Chapter 5

Life on the Streets

◆

September brought back a pool of volunteers well rested from their vacations and eager to work, many returning to the church dinner program sites that had reopened after Labor Day. Not having to worry about nightly cooking, daily shopping expeditions, and sweltering evenings hauling hot food from the shoebox kitchen meant more time to develop a social service program aimed at helping the women leave the shelter for permanent living situations. And I cannot say I was unhappy about the change for purely personal reasons. The increased personal time meant I could begin to look for my own apartment. I greatly looked forward to this because the long commute coupled with the long work hours was leaving me perpetually exhausted. I was fortunate to find another program staffperson with relative ease this time around. I interviewed a young woman named Vicki, asking her several questions relating to the job.

"Do you think any of your college coursework would be relevant to the job?" I asked, about midway through the interview.

A moment of hesitation, and then, "Is that a canned question?" I liked her immediately. She was direct and she had a sense of humor. Although Vicki had just graduated from college, with a psychology degree and a little volunteer experience in a soup kitchen, the level of maturity she displayed set her apart from other applicants who had little or no job experience. One sensed that she was very sensitive, while at the same time she seemed to be a tough, no-nonsense person. She would not be kicked around by the women, yet would undoubtedly win their trust with her easygoing manner and commonsense approach to problems. Vicki accepted the job with an agreement to start on the opening of the day program, just a few weeks away.

Day program volunteers had been recruited to help with the proposed group activities: Chandler was to handle job counseling, George an art group, Teresa housing information, Mary the community meeting, and Barbara a writing group. A mobile health/psychiatric team, comprised of an LPN and a psychiatric nurse, visited several different shelters each week, adding a weekly trip to the day program to their fall schedule. They were able to treat minor health problems, making outside referrals if more serious problems were identified, and to screen for psychiatric problems, prescribing psychotropic (antipsychotic) medications if deemed necessary, and if the woman was willing to accept treatment. Joan and I brought boxes of soup, canned foods, and office supplies to the church basement that would serve as the program space. We had use of this space Monday through Thursday only, necessitating the use of a different church basement on Friday. Different locations meant doing without vital file and resource materials on Friday, and for several months, operating without a telephone with an outside line. This was certainly not optimal, but we had to either make do or not do anything at all.

At the same time, members of the coalition's board of directors had been searching for a building to purchase as a permanent residence for people without homes. They found a single room occupancy (SRO) hotel for sale in the neighborhood and decided to buy it. Permanent housing would provide an actual solution to homelessness in addition to the band-aid emergency services that the coalition already supplied in conjunction with the settlement house agency. Emergency services were definitely needed, but without long-term solutions the problem of homelessness would remain a crisis.

The SRO the coalition had found was a seventy-room hotel. *Hotel* is a misleading term, because most of the people living in New York City's SROs were not travelers renting a room for the duration of a visit. SRO hotels were permanent living situations for the city's poor, rooms in them typically costing anywhere from thirty to eighty dollars per week. Lack of services, general lack of upkeep, violence, building violations, and filth were characteristic in these rundown buildings. The SRO the coalition planned to purchase was in need of major renovation, but was in relatively good condition for an SRO. Its biggest drawback was that it had no cooking facilities whatsoever (some SROs do). The coalition hoped to remedy this by eventually building a communal kitchen on the first floor. The rooms were quite small, ranging from six by nine feet to ten by twelve feet, with poorly functioning bathrooms in the halls, each to be shared by four or five rooms. Nirvana it was not, but considering the dearth of low-cost housing available, it began to look good.

In order to buy the building, the coalition had to raise close to one million dollars by the end of the year, roughly three months away. The board, with Pat the stalwart captain at the helm, decided to do it—not to *try* to do it, but to *do* it! The push began, with board members carrying out a carefully laid-out plan to scour the neighborhood, foundations, and corporations for donations. The women at the day program also helped by preparing large stacks of fund-raising literature for the mail. The day program had begun with only a few women but gradually had grown to include an average of ten women per day. Vicki and Joan had been spending a lot of time with the women and their individual case plans, and they had begun to make inroads with some of them.

With these projects well underway, and the dinner program and soup kitchens in full operation, we decided to do a little outreach to people in the neighborhood who were obviously living on the streets and who might be willing to avail themselves of these programs. Realizing that it normally took a long time to gain a street person's trust, we figured that if we started an outreach effort in October, we might convince a person or persons to come into the shelter or one of the other programs by December, banking on the

fact that when the cold weather came, people might be more willing to accept help. With the large amount of work we each had, we
wound up spending very little time on the streets, but we did make
contact with a few people.

◆

We soon found out that we were not the only ones who were
making such efforts. I came in to work one chilly morning in October to find a rather dramatic-looking person waiting for me in the
lobby. The first thing that struck me when I glanced over at her was
her hat. This little woman, wearing several layers of clothing and
a display of costume jewelry, was topped off with a large, burgundy picture hat, perched jauntily on her head. Beneath the rim
loomed oversized, rose-colored sunglasses. As I approached, she
smiled shyly and introduced herself as Suzanne. She had a heavy
French accent and a delicate manner of speech and movement.

"It is so kind of you to speak to me," she said, inclining her head
in an apologetic manner. "I have this to show you."

Typed on a plain white piece of paper were the words: "I am an
actress. You look like you may be in show business too. I would
like to help you. Renee Young."

"What is this?" I asked.

"A very nice lady, a Miss Renee, gave this to me in the park. She
has been talking to me and she told me to come here, that I could
get shelter, only my blood is so rich that I don't really need shelter,
only it is getting so cold outside that I said yes, that I would come,"
she said.

This was all a little more colorful than the average scenario. I
wondered who Renee Young was and whether she was truly an actress. I wondered who the lady beneath the hat and behind the
glasses was.

Suzanne came into my office for an intake interview. She was
very sweet, with a fragile, eggshell-like vulnerability.

"Where have you been living?" I asked.

"I live in the park, by the entrance on 79th Street," she said.
"That is where I met Miss Renee. She is always out walking her dog
and she started to talk to me."

"How long have you been living in the park?"

"Oh, I don't really know," Suzanne replied. "A long time. I was in a shelter for a little while, and then they accused me of vicious lies and I had to go, but I had nowhere to go so I went back to the park."

"What do you mean? You were thrown out of the shelter?"

"Yes. They were horrible! Terrible!" she lamented, a sobbing, panicky quality entering her voice. "I am a clean person. Why do they insult me and my rich blood? I am from King David. I am full of gold, and they . . . ."

I tried to interrupt her as she began to grow more hysterical and incoherent. I would learn that conversations with Suzanne never went very far before taking a swing into the no-man's-land of psychotic delusion.

"Suzanne, what was the thing that made them throw you out?" I asked.

"They accused me of crimes! Lies! I am a clean person . . . ."

"But what crime did they accuse you of?" I pressed, wondering if I would ever be able to get the straight story.

"They wanted me to take off my hat. They wanted me to lose my precious beauty," she sobbed.

"Why?" I asked. "Why did they want you to take off your hat?"

"Lice! Lice! They said I have lice under my hat."

Now we were getting somewhere.

"And did you have lice?" I asked.

"No," Suzanne said firmly. "I am clean. They just want to ruin me and my precious beauty. They want to kill me with their lies," she whimpered, exhausted by the emotional expenditure.

"So you started living in the park after that?"

"Yes, yes. It is okay. Only it is getting colder, and Miss Renee is very nice and told me you were nice here."

"Well, you don't need to be afraid here," I said, wondering again who Renee was. "It's safe, and we are here to try to help you."

"Thank you. You are very kind," she said.

"Where did you live before the other shelter?"

"I lived on Fifth Avenue by the Metropolitan Museum of Art, with a very nice man, Mr. Bergdal. But it was not sexual, because I am non-sex. Non-sin, non-sex, because I am filled with rich blood of King David, my mother. I am firstborn of my race and have the blood of gold flowing all through my non-sex body. I am non-sex with the rich blood of kings all over my body and that is why I am so rich and . . . ."

I had a feeling the energized, rapid flow of words could continue indefinitely, regardless of whether or not there was an audience for them. Fifth Avenue near the museum had some of the highest-priced living quarters in the city. I wondered if Suzanne had really lived there. It was curious, but not unlikely. I heard incredible stories almost every day, and most turned out to be true. She said she was staying in the park by 79th Street, which was not far from the museum and where her former apartment would have been. This was typical of many people who lost their apartments and then established new territories on the streets very close to their old homes.

I got what little other information I could from Suzanne, inviting her to stay at the shelter if she agreed to abide by our rules of regular bathing. She agreed, on the condition that she not be asked to remove her hat in public. I told her she could keep her hat on whenever she wanted, as long as she took it off to bathe. Agreed. Disheveled as she was, she appeared to be clean, giving credibility to her promise, especially given the fact that she had apparently found some way to bathe herself while living in the park.

A few days later, I was filled in on some of the key events in Suzanne's life. Renee Young phoned me to find out how Suzanne was doing. She really did exist!

Renee was indeed an actress, and a very popular one, having been the star of a soap opera for over twenty-five years. She lived very close to the entrance of the park where Suzanne used to live and had felt so saddened by seeing her there every day that she had been compelled to reach out and talk to her. The human bond of compassion cut across the illusory boundaries, and Suzanne eventually accepted food from Renee and her offer of friendship.

I was buoyed by Renee's good-hearted spirit. Coming across people like her made the city seem like a more intimate place. Renee filled me in on many missing facts about Suzanne's life that would help us begin to understand her, the first step in helping infuse some stability into her life again. Suzanne *had* lived with Mr. Bergdal on Fifth Avenue near the museum for twenty-five years.

Suzanne's mother was a French courtesan who became pregnant by an American soldier stationed in Europe during World War II. He never saw Suzanne. Thrown out by her mother when she was seventeen, Suzanne left Paris to come to the United States, where she soon met Mr. Bergdal, many years her senior. She lived with him until his death, four years ago. He left her all his savings: $90,000. Suzanne continued to live in their apartment while haphazardly spending every penny of her inheritance over a three-year period. She had been mentally ill for some time and had no conception of the value of money or budgeting; she bought what delighted her, like a child in a toy store.

At approximately the same time that Suzanne was spending the last of the money, the apartment became overrun by roaches, which began to infest the adjacent apartments. This prompted the management of the building to issue a letter to Suzanne stating that an exterminator would be coming the following week. Suzanne thought this meant that *she* was to be exterminated, so she immediately left the apartment, never to return again. That was one year ago.

Renee had gathered this information in snatches from Suzanne, and later corroborated it by talking to Jeff, a man Suzanne had asked Renee to contact for her. Jeff had been involved with the funeral arrangements for Mr. Bergdal and had befriended Suzanne, trying to prevent her from losing her home and money. His efforts to help her had not been enough to stop the process, and he had watched her losses mount over the years, first losing the most significant person in her life, then her money, finally her apartment, and with it all trace of stability. He had stored some of Suzanne's belongings for her at his home in Westchester county, hoping that someday, somehow, she would live under a roof again and could use these household items.

So there she was—alone, broke, scared. She could not comprehend why her life had changed so radically, so quickly; the confusion fed her psychotic delusions, and the cyclone kept spinning faster. Each day was a survival test, and one sensed that Suzanne lived in acute anxiety over whether she would pass the test or not. "Thank you for saving my life," she said when I had offered her the available shelter bed. She would recount on many occasions how I had "saved her life" on that day. I could only account for this by conjecturing that Suzanne must have felt very close to failing the test that day for her to have equated emergency shelter with life itself.

Suzanne spent most of her first night in the shelter sitting in a lounge chair, furiously writing on crumpled sheets of paper. She never went near her bed. In the many months and scores of nights she would spend in the shelter, she never did. Her furious writing was mostly illegible and insensible, relating to forces from outer space, her royal lineage, and how the world was out to annihilate her. One had to wonder if the latter musings made some logical sense, given her current situation.

◆

It was the beginning of a relationship with Suzanne, and as with each new shelter guest, we hoped we could work together towards increased well-being and ultimately towards finding a home. Sometimes it was easier to entertain hope for newcomers, harder to sustain hope for those who seemed to be making little apparent change over long periods of time. It was getting colder, and we were growing increasingly worried about Nancy. She was as unsteady on her feet as ever, teetering, tottering, turtling her way down the street to the corner McDonald's for lunch, then back to the steps to join Emma to sit, sit . . . sit. When winter's snow and ice came, we were afraid she would suffer bad falls and broken bones that are the nemesis of old age. Sitting outdoors all day in freezing temperatures could exacerbate her heart ailments as well. The day program presented a catch-22, because she could be indoors, but would have to first walk nine blocks to get there. But I was puzzled for quite some time about why she refused to go to the senior center, just two doors away from the shelter. I did not understand her resistance until she told me that she went there one afternoon and all the old people were friendly and asked where she lived, only to scoff and turn their backs on her when she told them the truth.

Though little outward change had taken place, we were pleasantly surprised to learn that internal changes had been going on. One morning, seemingly the same as all the others, Nancy announced that she was willing to move to a nursing home. She was ready.

Nursing home is actually a misnomer. Nursing homes are for people who require the presence of round-the-clock skilled nursing care. An individual could only get into a nursing home if she or he scored at least 160 on a DMS-1 form, the document that determined what level of nursing care an individual needed. The DMS-1 assigned scores to such things as the ability to feed oneself, use the bathroom alone, dress, walk, take medications, and so forth. Those who scored between 120 and 160 could not be admitted to a nursing home but were eligible for a bed in a health related facility (HRF). Nancy's DMS-1 score fell into this category. Daily care is provided at HRFs, but they do not have twenty-four-hour skilled nursing care. In other words, people are healthier and/or more independent at HRFs.

Joan began calling HRFs in the New York vicinity, asking for applications and information on the availability of a bed. The information was devastating; there were waiting lists of two to seven years. Two to seven years!! What was Nancy supposed to do in the meantime? I began helping Joan with the calls, hoping to be able to persuade an administrator to accept Nancy based on the severity of her circumstances. I truly believed she would not make it through the winter at the shelter, so I pleaded and begged. Nothing.

Then Maria thought of an idea. One of the social workers at the agency's community service department, Joanne, had formerly worked in a nursing home. Maria thought she might have some ideas about how to speed up the process or know of unlisted facilities we had not yet called. Connections work miracles. Joanne called her old boss and explained our dilemma. Nancy was promised one of their beds in a week, pending an intake interview. We were thrilled, but tried to curb our excitement, fearing that Nancy might change her mind about the whole thing. And she still had to pass the interview.

That week, Vicki borrowed her parents' car to drive Nancy to the Brooklyn home for the interview. Joan and I were at the day program when Vicki returned from the excursion, a big grin spread across her face. "She was accepted!" she exclaimed.

"She was? I can't believe it! What did she say? Is she going to do it?" we asked.

"Yes. It's all set for next Friday," Vicki answered. "Everything went great. She likes the place, the neighborhood's nice, there are trees all around, and she can even walk to the stores if she wants to. I couldn't believe it either. It all worked out so well."

We all felt *so good*. With casework with the women going so slowly, both because of resistance by some women as well as the absolute dearth of affordable housing, it was gratifying to see something work out for a change. A renewed sense of hope filled us and the other women as we shared in the pleasure of seeing someone move on to something better.

We helped Nancy gather her belongings during the week and tried to help her prepare for the psychological adjustment of leaving the shelter where she had lived for over a year. Each time we spoke with her she seemed quite prepared to go. It was as if once she had made the decision to leave she was at peace with it and with herself. Arrangements were made for our faithful volunteer, Mary, to drive Nancy and me to the home on Friday. We were planning to stop first at Nancy's bank, about ten blocks south of the shelter, to close out her savings account. Nancy received a relatively large Social Security check each month, because she had had fairly high paying jobs throughout her adult life, until she retired. The $7,000 in her account would pay for about the first two months in the HRF, after which she would have to apply for Medicaid, like every other senior citizen who exhausts his or her life savings at nursing homes and HRFs in the matter of a few months or a few years. Perhaps coming to terms with this financial arrangement could explain some of Nancy's initial resistance to considering a nursing home or HRF placement. Seeing the money earned during the course of a lifetime spent in a whisper of time can be a powerful source of dissuasion for many older people who might need a supportive residence but be afraid to enter one for fear of becoming a virtual pauper.

Friday morning arrived and everything was running smoothly. Mary pulled up to the shelter doors promptly at 10 A.M., we loaded the car and drove to the bank, Mary double-parking while Nancy and I went in. Nancy went to a counter and filled out the appropriate slips while I stood a couple of steps away.

"Okay. I think that's right," she said, turning towards the teller. With the turn, her left foot got caught on the leg of the counter and she did a pirouette-like movement before slamming to the marble floor. I gasped as I saw her body crumple. "My God, we almost made it! How can this happen?!" I thought frantically, trying to steady Nancy's flailing limbs as she searched for balance. After Nancy had suffered through living in the shelter for so long, after she had finally decided to accept what was probably her only reasonable housing option, after we had been fortunate enough to find a bed for her so quickly, avoiding years on a waiting list, could fate really be so cruel as to have allowed her to fall, less than an hour away from sealing the move? If she broke something, she would likely be hospitalized and the HRF bed would undoubtedly be given to someone who was ready to move in immediately. I felt profound disappointment.

"Can somebody help?" I asked with anger, looking at the ring of bodies forming around us, everybody gaping, no one moving to help. Someone from the bank finally came over and tried to help Nancy stand up.

"She may have broken something," I said, finding it hard to believe that the impact of such a fall would *not* have broken anything. "We'd better not move her."

True to form, Nancy insisted on getting to her feet, saying she was fine and remaining relatively calm. We helped her to a chair and someone brought her a cup of water. Relief rushed through me as I realized she was not seriously injured. After resting for five minutes, Nancy completed her business with the teller, and we gingerly made our way out of the bank. Mary pulled up minutes later, having had to circle around the block several times to avoid getting a parking ticket.

When we arrived at the HRF, the social worker greeted Nancy like an old friend, quickly taking her through the intake procedure. She then gave us a tour of the facility, which was indeed a nice place. I had been in many nursing homes and HRFs over the years, and the quality of service offered varied greatly. The thing that impressed me most about this HRF was that it did not smell! It always turned my stomach to enter a "home" to be assaulted by that hospital smell of heavy-duty cleaner, bedpans, and medicine. This place did not have an odor. It was clean and bright without having an institutional feeling to it, and the staff seemed caring and warm.

Nancy had given us all firm orders not to keep in touch with her. She wanted to "forget about that place." Mary and I wished her well and said goodbye, knowing we would miss her endearing personality, knowing she would not miss the invasion we represented to her. We had become uninvited participants in Nancy's life; she would have it back now, and she would try to erase the imprint caused by loss of her home.

Helping Nancy get out of the shelter gave Joan, Vicki, and me a big psychological boost. There *was* light at the end of the tunnel. The months and months of work we did with Nancy, and Nancy's months of struggle with herself, had paid off. Not only were we happy for Nancy, but it gave us hope that we would eventually see other efforts come to fruition, as we struggled to find ways to be supportive to these women who were harshly challenged physically and emotionally by living in the shelter, by living with the stigma of homelessness.

An unaffordable rent increase, a lover thrown out the door, a welfare center inexplicably cutting off one's payments—in the course of a few days one could find oneself walking into a shelter for the first time, then suffering a long stay before walking out for the last time. For someone who had recently lost her apartment, the biggest impediment to getting out of the shelter was usually finding another affordable apartment. Sadly, because there was so little affordable housing, healthy and motivated women were forced to remain in this "temporary" state of limbo for prolonged periods. Those who had spent time living on the street before coming to a shelter (perhaps because there had been so few shelters, and fewer still with available beds), usually already had a host of serious problems. Minor problems could only be exacerbated by living on the street. Street and shelter life exacerbated problems to such a degree that housing concerns were often overshadowed by the most basic needs of food, clothing, and shelter.

◆

Suzanne had been with us several weeks already, but was too fearful to take full advantage of the shelter, still refusing to sleep in or even go near her bed. Her delusions were such that she was in constant fear of being poisoned, so she refused any offers of food. Renee spent time with her during the day, trying to convince her to come off the rock that she had lived on in the park, to come to the day program where she could get lunch and begin to work with Joan on her case plan. Suzanne had agreed to go on several occasions, each time on the condition that Renee go with her. Although Renee was more than willing to oblige her, her work schedule did not allow her to do this often. Once at the day program, Suzanne still refused food, subsisting on the raw eggs that Renee began to supply her with. Raw eggs were the only food Suzanne would eat because they were the only food she could be certain no one had tampered with. Poking a small hole through the shell, Suzanne would suck the "pure" food down her throat.

Suzanne also insisted on dressing in a street person's typical mode of dress, including several layers of clothing and usually some type of hat. This choice of dress made sense for a person who lived on the street and had to depend on surviving through all types of weather with whatever was on one's back, or in the bags she could carry. However, once inside a shelter this manner of dress was not readily altered, for the sense of chronic insecurity and transience often remained a long time. As with Suzanne, her defenses would not allow her to let down her guard long enough to entertain the possibility that she might not need to keep this mobile refuge of layers with her at all times, that a return to the streets was not inevitable. It took time to build up such a fearful mentality; it took an even longer time to begin to chip it away.

◆

Occasionally, women would come and go before we had a clue as to who they really were, who the inner person beneath the worn exterior was. Irma was such a person. She breezed in and out towards the latter half of October. I saw her on my way to work one day, a half block away from the entrance to the shelter.

As I walked by, I noticed a person partially covered under a filthy blanket. Unfortunately, seeing half-frozen bodies huddled in doorways is not uncommon in New York City, so I did a double take only when I realized the person was a woman and that she might not know about our programs. I knelt down and introduced myself, telling her that I worked in a private shelter just a half block away and asking if she had spent the night on the street. Irma began to answer when a passerby, about fifty-five years old, well dressed and snippety-looking, stopped to peer at us.

"Why don't you just go with her?" she said in a condescending tone.

Irma looked at us with confused eyes.

"This nice lady will take you to the shelter. You shouldn't be out here on the street. Here, pick up your blanket and go with her," she carried on in her well-bred, disgusted, I-know-what's-good-for-you voice.

"Ma'am, thanks for your help, but I'd really like to talk to this woman alone, if you don't mind. It's okay—really. Thanks," I said, trying to be polite so she would go away without a fuss. Her superior attitude made my skin crawl. She "Hmphed" away.

"Anyway, did you spend the night outside?" I repeated.

"Yeah. I have no place to go," Irma muttered.

"Where did you sleep the night before last?"

"I was out by the park. Someone told me there was a shelter around here but I couldn't find it," she said dejectedly, pulling out a crumpled slip of paper from her pocket which had the settlement house name and address scrawled on it.

Irma agreed to come in for an intake interview. Within minutes, it became apparent that she was mentally ill, and possibly alcoholic as well. I felt a familiar sense of rage as I thought of the mental health system: the lack of community supports coupled with the hospitalization laws that help to keep someone like Irma on the street. During the interview, she said she had been discharged a few weeks earlier from a mental hospital in New Jersey. Though someone on the street had told her where our shelter was, she had spent yet another night on the sidewalk because she did not have the wherewithal to find the building, just a half block away from the spot where she lay. Her blanket and clothing were caked with urine. She was so physically exhausted that she fell off the chair, forming a heap on the floor.

If a child needs protection and support, she or he is bound by law to get it until reaching adulthood. Needy adults, like Irma, were given the "right" to care for themselves but few resources to do so. From a system that was once accused of locking people up unnecessarily, we have evolved to a point where liberty is heralded as the ultimate prize. But without the supports enabling that freedom to flourish, "freedom" often became an unwitting straitjacket of a different cloth.

So we gave Irma some clean clothes, she came to the shelter for two nights, and we never saw her again. Maybe she could not find her way back again. No one had time to reflect on the possibilities for too long. There were always more women asking for beds, more problems with the casework, and more crises. Every week or two the full horror of living without a home would smash into the illusory routine of daily life.

◆

Michelle, seemingly the least likely, was a near-casualty during those last weeks in October. Our resident pâté lover, Michelle had held a prestigious administrative job for a renowned orchestra for close to twenty-five years, leaving with letters of recommendation from some of the foremost musicians in the United States. She had chosen to leave her job in order to pursue a lifelong dream of involvement in the art world.

A well-educated woman with an intellectual bent, she had learned that it was more difficult than she had anticipated for a middle-aged woman to make a career change. What she had not been willing to do, and was still not willing to do, was to take an entry-level job. Since she had earned over $30,000 in the past, she felt it was beneath her to stoop to take a job which paid only $10,000 to $15,000 a year. Strangely enough, she was more willing to become and remain homeless than compromise on this issue. It was less strange if one took into account that the difficulties associated with the job change rendered her depressed, and depression can alter a person's decision-making process radically.

Michelle had been at another private shelter for over a year before coming to us. She had actually been both client and staff at that shelter, working as a housemother, from what I understood. She seemed to have been willing to perform the housemother duties because psychologically she did not consider this to be a real job. It was merely a means of survival. However, the shelter was not looking for a permanent resident. When it became apparent that Michelle was doing little to look for work outside the shelter, they reminded her that they were running an emergency shelter, not a long-term residence. As the months turned into a year and there had been no change in Michelle's pursuits, the shelter staff asked her to leave. She had moved into the settlement house shelter, arriving several months before I had started work there.

Michelle had unemployment checks coming in every two weeks, the last check to cover the two weeks ending on October 25th. We had been helping her prepare for a job search: updating her resume, getting monetary donations so she could buy an interview outfit that did not look like someone's ill-fitting hand-me-down, hooking her up with a volunteer who worked in a personnel agency who was willing to set up interviews, offering encouragement. We also set limits in an effort to provide incentive for her to overcome her depression and to keep trying. Michelle had to check the want ads every day, go to employment agencies, and follow through with any job interviews that were offered to her, or we would terminate her stay.

Michelle was acquiescing, but very reluctantly, frequently making outrageous excuses to try to avoid interviews, and looking for every opportunity to blame *us* for her situation. Michelle blamed being unemployed and without a home on everyone but herself, adopting a look-what-you (the staff, the employment agencies, her former employers, the world)-have-done-to-*me* attitude. I conjectured that Michelle's confidence had been shattered so severely that she was petrified to face rejection on job interviews, seeking someone or something to blame so she would not have to face her fear. She wanted to back out of her relationship with the world.

As the end of October neared, Michelle was becoming increasingly morose, talking even less to those around her. She refused to go into formal counseling, continuing to deny that she had any problems and accusing everyone around her for holding her back. Any vitality that she used to possess was draining away as she withdrew into her shell. Joan and Vicki had been spending a lot of energy and time trying to reach her, becoming worried when the withdrawal process proceeded unabated. On October 23rd, I talked to Michelle at the dinner program to try to understand what was going on, to try to figure out how we could help her. Becoming frustrated with our conversation, I tried to press Michelle to deal with reality instead of giving me "that's your problem" responses and meandering around in vagueness.

"Michelle, your unemployment runs out in two days. You know you could apply for an extension. You refuse to do this, yet you do not seem to be genuinely interested in getting a job, and I want to know why," I said.

"Don't you know?" she asked with an attitude suggesting that I was an imbecile.

"No, I don't. Why don't you tell me?" I asked.

"Why do you think I wouldn't care whether or not I got the unemployment benefits any more?" she needled.

"I honestly don't know, Michelle. That's why I'm asking you," I said with failing patience.

"I won't need it if I won't be here anymore."

Thud. I hoped she was not trying to tell me what I thought she was.

"What do you mean you won't be here anymore?" I asked.

"I simply won't be here," she responded arrogantly.

"Well where are you going?" I asked, pretending not to catch on, in the hope that my hunch was wrong.

"Where could I possibly go with no money?" she coaxed.

"I suppose you could go to another shelter, or maybe to a friend's house."

"I'm not going to another shelter, and I'm not going to a friend's. That doesn't leave very much, does it?" she asked.

"Michelle, I'm not here to play games. Are you trying to tell me you are thinking of committing suicide?"

"That is the logical step, isn't it?" she asked, her voice more tense now, lips tightly pursed, head cocked to one side. "No one here has helped me, what else is there for me to do?"

There it was. We talked further, as I tried to assess whether there was imminent danger of a suicide attempt, drawing upon prior experiences I had had with suicidal clients at previous jobs. Michelle seemed to be very clear about the October 25th deadline (two days away), so I felt there was no immediate danger of an attempt. My instincts told me that she was rather uncertain about the whole thing, but when anyone comes near the subject of suicide, one has to take any threat very seriously. An incorrect assessment can mean death.

I called the health team the next day for a psychiatric consultation. They told me what I expected to hear: if she were still talking about suicide that day, I should call the police and have her taken to the emergency room for an evaluation, even if there were a large margin of doubt. No chances should be taken.

That night, I went to the dinner program again and spoke with Michelle. Her story was the same. I told her that if she was really serious about considering suicide, I was professionally obliged to try to get her psychiatric help. She shrugged indifferently. I felt very awkward. To witness, through some exchange of words and motions, someone relinquish responsibility over her own life! To witness someone essentially saying, "I cannot handle the pain of being in the world. I'm leaving."

Yet I still did not have the gut feeling, which I had experienced before with suicidal people, that Michelle was serious about following through with her threat. But this was a judgment call that the emergency room personnel had to make, not me. If she did not appear to have crossed the bridge between contemplation and action, a hospital emergency room would not admit her. Involuntary commitment for suicidal or homicidal people on the "threshhold" was not legally allowed. I wondered which way it would go.

After dinner, we walked the few blocks to the shelter.

"Michelle, have you thought about *how* you're going to commit suicide?" I asked. This is a stock question for counselors. People who have carefully laid-out plans are much more apt to go through with a suicide attempt than those who only have a vague notion of "ending it all."

"What kind of a sick mind do you have?" she exploded, sputtering out the words in anger. "You want to know how and when? Do you want to watch? I've told you I'm doing it. Isn't that enough?"

"I only asked because I wanted to figure out just how serious you are about this. I already told you I'm obliged to make you see a psychiatrist now, even if it has to be against your will. Do you understand that?" I asked.

"Do what you have to do," she said glumly.

"Will you come with me to the emergency room now?" I asked.

"No."

"If you won't go with me, I'll have to have you taken forcibly. I hate to do this, but you leave me no choice," I said.

In a few hours it would be October 25th, the day she said she would "leave."

"Go ahead," she said quietly, and went into the shelter.

I dreaded making the call to the police. I knew Michelle already felt a keen sense of degradation because of her circumstances, and this would make it worse. Yet it was something that had to be done, and we both knew it. I called the precinct number and explained the situation. We were fortunate to be in a very responsive precinct. The police usually showed up quickly and treated the women with respect.

They came within minutes, only in greater number than I had anticipated. Four uniformed policemen showed up at the front door to the building, as I had requested, rather than at the side entrance to the shelter. I let them in and explained the situation again, careful to stress that Michelle was not a volatile individual. Three of them stayed at the doorway, the fourth seating himself on a couch as I asked Michelle to come into the lobby area where we would have privacy. She calmly came in, looking curiously at the police, and seating herself next to the officer on the couch.

"I called the police to ask that they take you to the hospital emergency room," I said.

"Why? Nothing's wrong with me," she said in a controlled manner.

"Ma'am, I understand that you are thinking of committing suicide. We don't want that to happen. We want to help you get help," the police officer said.

"Why do you think I want to commit suicide?" Michelle asked. "I never said a word about that to you."

"Miss Ferrill told me you had spoken about it with her," he said.

"That's none of your business," Michelle said, with a touch of alarm creeping into her voice. "I told her that, I didn't tell you."

"Michelle, I told you I would have to force you to get help if you didn't do it voluntarily," I said. "We just don't want to see you hurt yourself."

"What I do is my business. Nobody asked you to get involved," she said.

"Whether you asked me to or not, I am involved. And I can't stand around and watch you kill yourself."

"Well, I'm sorry. I'm not going," she said, heading back into the shelter.

"Ma'am, you don't understand," the officer said, catching up with her. "I *have* to take you to the hospital. Why don't you come with us voluntarily? You can talk to the psychiatrist at the hospital and see what he has to say. They're only there to help."

"Well, I don't want any help, and I'm simply not going," she replied.

"Then I'm sorry, Ma'am, but we're going to have to cuff you," he said, pulling handcuffs out of his pocket.

A look of fear and confusion swept across Michelle's face. It was not that she did not understand what was happening; it was as if her logic simply would not comprehend that this was happening to her.

"Michelle, please just go. Don't make him put handcuffs on you," I implored.

In response, Michelle made a dash for the door, prompting the other policemen to step in and hold her arms while the officer we had spoken with handcuffed her wrists behind her back. Michelle's pale white face had a look of abject humiliation. It was a horrible sight. Despair hung in the air. I asked one of the volunteers scheduled for the night to accompany Michelle to the hospital to make sure she was treated well, to give her moral support, and in case the hospital did not admit her, to accompany her back to the shelter.

Two and one half hours later, Gina telephoned me at home. Michelle and the volunteer had returned. After waiting over two hours to be seen, Michelle met briefly with the psychiatrist, told him she did not intend to commit suicide, and was released. I did not know whether I was relieved or not. Was she bluffing all along, perhaps to get attention? Had she really been unsure, this episode forcing her to make a concrete decision? Was she fooling the doctor in order to be released, in which case suicide might still be a threat?

It had been my experience in the past that when people are contemplating suicide, they are relieved when someone reaches out to intervene and would reach for the lifeline. My best guess was that Michelle had been toying with the idea of suicide, but when the chips were down, she realized she did not want to go through with it. She chose life.

When I spoke to Michelle the next day, she said she was not going to do anything to hurt herself. I said that she seemed depressed, suggesting she might feel better if she went to formal counseling. Michelle denied feeling depressed. She blamed the shelter for her situation, saying we had done nothing to help her. When I pointed out all the ways we had offered assistance and asked what more we could do for her, she looked taken aback. "Pâté! Give me the pâté I need," she said, as if this response was painfully obvious.

Pâté. It was baffling. This very intelligent, cultured, educated woman, who had held a very responsible job for twenty-five years, had been married, widowed, and currently spent her free time at the day program listening to symphonic tapes, doing *The New York Times* crossword puzzles, and reading the newspaper every day to keep her mind stimulated, was telling me the key to her peace of mind was pâté. Was it the initial trauma of not finding employment that had defeated her? Was it her inability to continue paying her rent, her eviction from her comfortable apartment that had done it? Was it shelter life that had finally, and seemingly wholly, defeated her?

I searched my mind in vain for the key, as I wheeled my shopping cart through the supermarket.

I threw some pâté into the cart.

Chapter 6

Throwing People Out

♦

I pulled my winter coat close to shield myself from the November wind as I walked across town to get to work. After months of searching, I had finally moved into a one-bedroom apartment with my college roommate, Vivian. She had graduated from Harvard Business School in the spring and was to begin work at a bank in New York City. The apartment was in a glittering highrise, with a doorman, in a yuppie neighborhood. We partitioned off part of the living room to serve as my bedroom. I did not like feeling like the poor church mouse: contributing less to the rent and bringing secondhand furniture, but my money was so tight. After paying $525 towards the $1,200 rent, and after taxes were taken out of my pay, I had $13 left a day for food, transportation, clothing, entertainment—and everything else. It frustrated me that a master's degree, very hard work, and doing something I felt was valuable to society in general was given relatively little monetary reward, but

I knew what I was getting into when I went into social work so I could not complain.

To make some extra spending money, I occasionally did modeling jobs in what little spare time I had. Besides a few extra dollars, these jobs also provided me with a sort of fantasy escape from the dismal reality of the shelter. I had other escapes, too, because Dennis was a great support in my life. A sensitive, thoughtful man, he was always willing to discuss concerns I had, unlike many other people who felt homelessness was too depressing to talk about. Since he lived in Boston, the time we spent together on his trips to New York was especially savored. When Dennis was in town, we saw the nice side of the city. He took me to elegant restaurants, jazz concerts, dancing, carriage rides through the park. I often thought of how those releases saved my sanity, gave me balance. Releases the women who had to deal with homelessness twenty-four hours a day, day after day, did not have.

As I approached the shelter, I wondered how much longer Emma and Louise could continue to sit on the shelter steps all day. Emma sat on the top step, wrapped in blankets or huddled under an umbrella, from 7A.M. until 10 P.M. without fail. Louise joined her in between brief walks around the neighborhood.

There had been no visible change with either of them. Emma still refused all offers of assistance. Perhaps this dismal way of life was comforting simply because it was dependable. Perhaps Emma had experienced such bad luck that she could only assume more catastrophes were a step away. I wished there were some way of knowing, some key that would unlock her. I had my own frustration to deal with, and every week at least one passerby would come into the agency to chastise me, as if I had somehow assumed sole responsibility for her.

"How can you let that poor old lady sit out there in the cold? Why aren't you doing anything to help her? This is an outrage!"

One day, a doctor from the hospital where Emma had been a nurse stopped in to talk to me. He was aghast to see her sitting on the shelter steps. I thought he might be able to help us understand Emma better, but instead he walked out of my office in a practically dazed state of disbelief.

Louise's resistance was even more frustrating. She had begun to emit an odor that grew more potent each day. She still refused to shower. One day Jean came to me in a furor because the odor coming from Louise, whose bed was next to her own, was making it difficult for her to sleep. She demanded action. Jean said the odor smelled like it came from an infection, and Jean was usually right about such things.

Sure enough, when I spoke to Louise, there was a stench from her right foot. Louise refused to discuss it. What should I do? Throw her out for having a stinking, infected foot? Make her go back to the streets where she was originally found, covered with filth? Or let everyone suffer, barely able to breathe? Yes, she should have been showering, but she was not. Should I toss her out as if she were some disposable that no longer functioned properly? I had no answer. I only knew I did not want to make that decision.

I decided to have a community meeting that night in an effort to use peer pressure to get Louise to bathe. Everyone assembled around a table. After a few minor agenda items, I brought up showering and how it was important for the community for everyone to comply. Several women picked up my lead and began discussing how particularly important cleanliness was with such close living arrangements. Louise had popped out of her seat and was shuffling around the lounge area.

"Louise, come sit with us. This is important. We're discussing showers," I said.

"Oh yeah? What kind of showers? Baby showers? That's nice," she said coyly.

She infuriated me! But at the same time, I had to squelch the urge to laugh. She surprised me with her sense of humor. I think she knew she was upsetting me and injected that humor not to make me mad, but to make me laugh. We all need to laugh at ourselves and our situations from time to time and it was nice to be reminded of that.

Louise never did join the table, and she still refused to bathe. I had to do the thing I hated: give her an ultimatum. I decided it was counterproductive to tell her to shower or leave the shelter. She was simply too likely to choose the street and stay there indefinitely. So I softened the choice; either shower or not be allowed in the sleeping room because the smell disturbed the others. In effect, this meant shower or sleep sitting on the floor of the lounge (we removed the chairs). She chose the floor.

The next morning, Gina said Louise went back to her bed in the middle of the night and Gina did not stop her for fear of disturbing all the other women. That night, we removed her mattress. The following morning, Gina told me Louise slept on the bedframe.

"What do you mean, Gina? She slept on the metal springs?"

"Yes, ma'am. She lay there with her back right on it," Gina said.

"Did she have a blanket or anything?" I asked.

"Nope."

Louise certainly was a tough little woman, but this could not continue. Even with Louise in the lounge area, the other women were still disturbed by the odor and Gina was threatening to quit if she had to sit in the same room with Louise, claiming she could not breathe all night. An odor from an infection has a distinct, sickening quality to it, and each day it became more intense. I told Gina I would have Louise stay in the small lobby area by the shelter entrance, which was closed off by doors. I did not want to give up and throw her out. I did not want to believe it was hopeless.

We decided to bombard her with as much attention as we could, to try to convince her to accept help. Each day, Vicki devoted a large portion of her time to try to break through Louise's resistance. The health team made a special trip to the shelter steps twice a week to try to coax Louise into letting them treat her foot, checking for any signs of gangrene. (Since the infection did not appear to be life-threatening, they could do no more than encourage her to accept treatment.) Volunteers talked to her. I talked to her. We hoped the bombardment approach would work, that all that consolidated attention and energy had to have some type of effect. Any effect had to be positive, because, short of her leaving, the situation was already about as bad as it could get, and if she did not get her bed back soon she was likely to leave anyway. After ten days of talking, Vicki scratched the surface.

Louise told her she feared taking a shower because the innermost layer of her stockings—she wore several pairs of foot and leg coverings—was stuck to the infection and she was afraid removing it would cause pain. Apparently, the infection was giving her a lot of pain as it was.

After Vicki got that wedge in and began to understand where the fear was coming from, things moved more quickly. Over the course of the following week, she and the health team got Louise to shower and peel off all layers but the last on the infected foot. The health team gave her an ointment which she put on and around the infected area, letting it seep through the stocking. It was an imperfect method, but it did the job. Louise agreed to put on a fresh set of clothes from the donation closet, and looked and smelled a lot better. She got the bed back.

The day after Louise bathed, Vicki came to work in a euphoric mood. I had not been there the night before, and did not yet know the news.

"Louise took a shower!" Vicki exclaimed. "I can't believe how excited I am over it. This is ridiculous. My roommate thinks I'm crazy. I was so psyched when I went home last night, and she asked me what was up. When I told her Louise had showered she thought I was nuts. I mean, who freaks out because somebody's showered? I'm telling you, this job is crazy. Everything takes on a new perspective."

That was certainly true. Every tiny step became a major cause for celebration. Between combatting the complex, sluggish, frequently antagonistic system, and trying to motivate people who, for a variety of reasons, had given up trying, progress was slow. Even when someone took a positive step, we knew we might not be able to keep up the support the person might need to maintain it. The hours spent in accomplishing that one small victory—just getting Louise to bathe! Hours, energy, patience, and compassion, largely from Vicki, had been necessary, and it would be impossible to devote that much energy and time to Louise indefinitely. We could not afford to do it. We had to provide services to the eighteen other women at the shelter, as well as the women at the dinner and day programs, and the walk-ins and the phone-ins. The level of support Louise would need to prevent her from slipping back into the danger zone was probably more than we could give her. It was hard enough trying to prevent physically and mentally healthy women from deteriorating when they lived without a home. With Louise, who was already debilitated, I felt we were trying to push her upwards towards physical and mental health while the shelter system was pushing down at the same time, grinding death and decay into her.

At least Louise's foot was on the mend, she was clean, and she had a bed. One day at a time.

And each day brought us closer to permanent housing. The coalition's board was frantically engaged in fund-raising, soliciting donations from neighbors, foundations, and religious organizations, and digging deeply into their own pockets. With the proposed closing on the SRO a month and a half away, several hundred thousand dollars were still needed. As money continued coming in daily, everyone involved shared the spirit. It *had* to be done. I hung on to that thought. Some of the women would finally get out of the shelter.

Beth, Gloria, and Lily broke my heart. They were so old! I would look at them, all seventy-five years old or older, shuffling around the crowded shelter, climbing the long flight of stairs to the shower, walking with canes, walking with pain, spending each night with eighteen strangers in a grim hall on a thin cot. No privacy, too few hours to sleep, little dignity. Respectful and respectable as they could have been, the situation stripped them of the external dignity they were due. They were not irresponsible people, they were not insane, they were not severely disabled — they just needed a place to live. And they were old. They were tired. I hoped they could continue to hang on until the building was bought.

Actually, it was amazing to witness the resiliency of the human spirit. Beth consistently amazed me. Seventy-eight years old, tiny and frail with a painful sciatic back problem, she walked thirty blocks each way every weekday to do volunteer work at a religious center after morning Mass, sorting and segregating donated clothing and other items to be sent throughout the city. Beth had been widowed at fifty-five, after what she described as an idyllic marriage of fifteen years to a doctor. She lit up when she spoke of him and their shared love, telling stories of particularly enjoyable evenings they had had with friends and of quiet countryside trips the two of them had taken. One sensed the void his death had created, though she only voiced thankfulness for their time together. When Beth's savings became depleted many years after her husband's death, Beth had to rely on her monthly Social Security check and was forced to move into a boarding house. One winter during a cold snap Beth took in for a few nights a homeless woman whom she had befriended on the street. The management of the boarding house discovered that she had an extra person in her room and threw her out for breaking house rules. She came to the shelter after being unable to find another affordable room.

That was almost two years ago.

Yet, despite her awful circumstances, Beth survived in body, mind, and spirit. She thrived on being charitable, giving of herself to as many she could: kind words, an understanding ear, money from her check to help other women who ran out by month's end, help around the shelter and the dinner program. Once I found a long-stemmed pink rose on my desk with a card, from Beth, who gave me the gift because she thought I had been looking tired and needed cheering up. She, who walked thirty blocks in pain to save the price of bus fare, spent her money to buy me a flower. Beth was an inspiration to my deflated spirit on many occasions.

◆

And God knows, spirits often needed a good blast of inflation. Shortly after Thanksgiving, a volunteer brought in a homeless woman she had met on the street—Hannah. I was thrilled. I had met Hannah on one of the few outreach walks I had made around the neighborhood over a month and a half ago. She had been huddled among at least twenty bags, the contents of which one could only imagine. Though I told her about the shelter and other programs, she had said she would not leave her neighborhood, just ten blocks south. She referred to the block she was camped out on as her home, having lived in an apartment on that block for over twenty years. She was somewhat disoriented and confused as to why she had been evicted, but I had been able to discern that she was thrown out over a year earlier, got a disability check each month, and had a nephew who sometimes gave her the additional money she needed to afford a hotel room for a few weeks out of the month.

And now she was in the shelter. I was glad that the outreach efforts of this volunteer had been successful in bringing her in off the street. Hannah was cold and hungry, so I made a hot cup of instant soup in the kitchen while the volunteer helped her adjust to being indoors, talking to her softly and reassuringly. After Hannah finished the soup and had warmed up, I explained the setup of the shelter and the few basic rules: no drugs or alcohol, no threats of violence of any kind, and regular bathing. When I tried to show Hannah where the shower room was we came to a halt. She did not think she could make it down the stairs. It was only then that I noticed the extent of her disability.

Hannah was under five feet tall with a rounded back that stooped to the right, limited movement in her right arm, and a painful leg that dragged behind her. Although Hannah made an effort to conceal her right hand, she eventually consented to opening the closed fist, exposing an ugly red gash through the center of her palm which was covered with grime and dust.

"Has a doctor or nurse ever looked at that hand?" I asked.

"No, no. It's nothing. It's okay, it doesn't bother me, really. I just have to be careful with it," she said unconvincingly in gruff, hushed tones, looking down to avoid meeting my eyes, a mannerism I would become well accustomed to.

"It's in a sensitive area. It might get infected," I said. I knew we would have to take it very slowly so she would not feel threatened. I suggested that she wash her hand and gave her some disinfectant, figuring that I would broach the subject of treatment when she was more settled. We still had to tackle the issue of her bags. Somehow she had consolidated the litter of shopping bags I had seen her with on the street into three hefty garbage bags, which the volunteer had helped her lug over. They smelled.

"I'm sorry to tell you this but we don't have room here for you to keep all these things," I said. "We have very little shared locker space."

"I know. I know it's a lot," Hannah replied. "I can get rid of a lot of stuff. I just need time to go through it all. I haven't been feeling well and I couldn't do it, but if you just let me rest tonight I'll work on it tomorrow," she said.

It seemed a reasonable request. She was obviously completely exhausted, every word she said barely audible, her body unable to hold itself upright in the chair. The bags seemed minor compared to the big step she had taken in coming in off the street. But I had learned from experience that I could not be too lenient or chaos would prevail.

"Okay, we'll let it go for tonight, but tomorrow you've got to go through them. I'll find a temporary place for them for tonight only. It wouldn't be fair to the other women to allow you more space, and besides that, I don't like the way these bags smell," I said. "They've been outside for a long time. You really need to go through them." I did not blame her for having dirty bags. She was doing her best to survive in a world she no longer understood. But

I had to make her understand what the reality of living in the shelter was, and dealing with the bags was part of that.

Having gotten her word to sort through the bags the next night and that she would give herself a thorough sponge bath later that evening, I let her rest in the chair in the lounge until the shelter opened. That night, I introduced her to Gina, Vicki, and the volunteers before leaving.

The next morning, reading the aides' nightly log, I was startled to learn that at 8:00 A.M. Gina had called the police to have Hannah removed from the building. Gina was supposed to have all the women out by 7:00 A.M., then clean up and clock out by 7:30. Hannah had gone into the bathroom, supposedly to wash, at 6:00 A.M. She told Gina she was too exhausted to do it the night before, and then refused to come out. When the morning began to wear on, Gina still could not convince her to come out of the bathroom. She got fed up and called the police to have Hannah forcibly removed.

I was upset for two reasons. First, I feared Hannah might be truly unable to comprehend what the rules of the house were, so that we might not be able to let her stay at the shelter. Second, I feared that Gina might be on the verge of no longer being able to perform her job adequately. Calling the police was a last resort, to be used only if the situation seemed threatening. To call the police on a new shelter guest for not leaving the bathroom showed very poor judgment, to put it mildly. I understood that Gina wanted to go home and that she genuinely did not know how to persuade Hannah to leave the bulding. What I did not understand was why she did not call me, or check to see who else was in the building who might be able to help her, such as my supervisor, Maria, who had come in before 8:00 A.M. I wondered if the stress of the job was becoming too much for Gina and hoped she would discuss her feelings openly when I talked to her that night. Meanwhile, I hated to think of what this action did to Hannah's view of the shelter and whether she would return. My bet was that she would. We still had her bags.

When we opened the shelter doors that night, she was there, full of apologies. Hannah said she was suffering from a stomach virus that morning and had had severe diarrhea, which she was still suffering from. In turn, I apologized for the way the incident had been handled. I also explained to her why we had to have certain rules, trying to impress upon her that an occasional emergency was acceptable, but that the shelter would not be allowed to operate if exceptions to the rules happened too often. Too many other programs depended on it, and the other shelter guests relied on communal respect of the rules as well.

I was frustrated. Though I was happy Hannah had come in off the street, I suspected that the shelter was an emergency bandage that would not bind the wounds for long. It was inadequate to meet her most rudimentary needs.

I left for the night, leaving Hannah in front of the bags to be sorted. The volunteers and Vicki prepared to help her consolidate her bags and take a sponge bath, as she had promised. The following morning I read the log. Things had gotten progressively worse. Despite the efforts of Vicki and the others, Hannah had refused to clean up her bags or to bathe. That was troublesome enough, but now she had begun saving the soiled bathroom tissue she used in the toilet, stashing it in the pockets of her oversized coat and in the cuffs of her pants. Gina, already beyond her endurance, reported that she could not bear the stench emanating from Hannah and demanded something be done.

Hannah had again claimed she was too physically ill to take care of cleaning herself or the bags. The few hours of rest at the shelter did not allow her to regain her strength. Of course this was true. After living on the street for months and years, interrupted by an occasional stint in a shelter, she was in an extremely weakened condition. Hannah was dying a slow and painful death. But deference to everyone else at the shelter did not allow me to wait for her to regain strength at their expense.

I discussed the situation with Maria and Paul, and we agreed on a plan to resolve the dilemma. If Hannah could sleep longer and not be on the street in the day (the day program was too far for her to walk with her disability), the rest might help her recuperate enough to bathe and sort her bags. To this end, the agency was willing to pay for a room at the YMCA for Hannah for three nights, at twenty-five dollars a night. If during that time Hannah repacked her bags, bathed, and agreed to see a doctor to determine the nature of the virus, both for her sake and that of the other women, she could come back to the shelter. The plan had a small chance of working. Since there were no other options, we figured it was worth a shot.

Hannah was not hard to find. She was sitting on a bench in front of the senior center two doors down from the shelter. I proposed the plan to her, and discussed it at length to make sure she understood what we were offering and why. Hannah agreed to it quite readily, saying in her soft-spoken and distracted manner that all she needed to clean herself and sort through her bags was to rest for a few days. She also reluctantly agreed to see a doctor. I went back to my office to arrange for the room and to see if I could get a volunteer to drive us there, since the bags would not fit into a taxicab's trunk.

Mary and her husband, Mike, were home and willing to help. They were the type of people I could always count on, even if the task was particularly unpleasant. This definitely fell into that category. Transporting someone with coat pockets stuffed with feces-covered tissues, her garbage bags filled with odorous, unknown materials, could not be construed as a pleasant way to spend an afternoon. Their large station wagon would make the job easier.

That done, I reserved a room for Hannah at a YMCA that I knew was clean and well-run, and was only two blocks away from my apartment. I decided to wait until the next day to try to find a doctor to examine Hannah, giving her a chance to rest and me a chance to assess whether she would in fact be willing to go through with an examination. After picking up the check to cover the room costs from the accounting office, we were ready to go.

Mike double-parked while Mary hopped out to help Hannah and me drag the enormous bags to the curb. We hoisted them into the back of the station wagon, rolled down the windows for air and headed to the Y. Upon arrival, I suggested we leave the bags by the door so the management would not throw us out before we even had a chance to check in. Mary watched the bags while Hannah and I went to the registration desk. Since the check was from the agency, I had to countersign for the room, explaining to the desk employee that we could only cover payment for the room for three days. We hustled the bags into the elevator and hurried up to Hannah's room. The room was small, but very clean. Hannah appeared relieved to be there. The bathroom and shower rooms were in the hallway, shared by the other women on the floor. I inspected them and found them to be immaculate and quite large. After going over the conditions one more time, I told Hannah I would stop by the next day to see how she was doing and to talk to her about the doctor's appointment.

The following day, I waited until the late afternoon before going to the Y so that Hannah would have had time to sleep late and get a start on things. When she opened the door to her room, she seemed to be in a dazed state. She had slept in her clothes, had not bathed, and her bags were exactly where I had left them.

"Hannah, what's going on?" I asked.

"I don't know. I just need some time, that's all," she muttered. "I have to organize my bags. I don't even know what's in there anymore," she continued, half mumbling to herself.

"Why don't we start now?" I suggested. "I can help you while I'm here."

"No, no. I need to lay everything out. I just need to rest."

"I know you're still tired, but unfortunately we can't pay for you to stay here for more than three days. That was the agreement. We normally don't put people up in rooms at all. We just don't have the money to do that. So we don't have a lot of time to work with and you need to go through the bags and wash yourself."

"I know," she said lamely. "I just need to rest."

"I know you do," I responded. "And I wish we could put you up here longer, but we can't. You've got to wash up. You can be carrying around a lot of germs at this point. At least start by throwing away those dirty tissues."

"Oh, they're not dirty. I may need them."

"You won't need them. You're in a room with a bathroom down the hall. There's plenty of clean tissue there. And you won't need them in the shelter either. Now come on. If you don't clean up I can't let you come back to the shelter, and I don't want to see you on the street again."

"I'm going to do it," she said. "I may need more time. I've been trying to reach my nephew to see if he'll loan me some money to stay here longer. Sometimes he loans me money," she said, nodding her head from side to side.

I accompanied Hannah to the lobby, where she called her nephew on the pay phone, leaving a message with his secretary. I promised to come back the next day, and left with a heavy heart. We had not even begun to discuss the physical examination. If I could not persuade her to bathe, chances were good that she would not see a doctor either. As usual, I tried to tune out my discouragement as I went home for the day, telling myself that tomorrow might bring a change for the better.

But tomorrow came and nothing had changed. This would be Hannah's last paid night at the Y, and she was in the same condition as when we brought her there. We talked. And talked. I pleaded with her. She spoke in vague terms of how she would be all right if only she could get through to her nephew. I suspected that he might be purposely evading her calls, although I did not say this to Hannah. I asked her if she would let me try to contact him, but she would not. I contemplated making a breach of ethics by calling him without her consent in order to determine if there were any family resources or information that I could use to help her, but I did not even know his full name.

We played the act over and over, each anticipating the other's lines. Did she understand this was the last night the agency had paid for and we could pay for no more nights? Did she understand that she could come back to the shelter only after bathing, sorting through the bags, and seeing a doctor? Did she understand it was freezing outside? Did she understand that I was sorry this was how it worked out? That I knew she was sick and exhausted and that the shelter offered her far less than a home? Far less than what anyone could get excited about? That I knew she was expecting to get her old apartment back some day? But that was not going to happen.

The story is predictable from there. Maybe it was predictable from the start, but I had wanted to believe we could change it. The Y's manager called the next day to tell me that Hannah had gone but that her bags were still in the room, and she wanted to know what to do. I explained the situation, and she generously offered to store Hannah's bags for a few days in case she came back for them. The following day, the manager called again to tell me that Hannah was found sleeping in a bathroom stall at the Y. She had slept there overnight. The manager wanted me to know that she was sorry, but she was going to have to throw her out. She did, and Hannah curled up on the sidewalk near the entrance to the Y.

I called an outreach team that covered that part of the city to see if they would visit the sidewalk and try to work with her. I was speaking on the day program's only telephone, which offered no privacy, because everyone was in the one room and could hear the conversations. Suzanne was sitting near the desk, heard my conversation, and began sobbing.

"You are trying to rob her of her freedom! She is free! She is free!

It is horrible what you are doing. Leave her to live in freedom, beauty." I could not understand. Suzanne had seen Hannah – confused, physically ill, filthy, alone.

"Suzanne, why do you think it is better that she be left in so-called freedom? How is she free? She's sick, she's freezing, she has nothing to eat, no place to go." I wanted Suzanne to understand me, she wanted me to understand her, but we could no longer communicate. She began to wail, describing the woes of living with the gold of King David flowing through her body, me growing silent, mystified, frustrated with my inability to empathize with Suzanne's definition of freedom, frustrated with my inability to make her understand that Hannah was not free to live if she was not healthy enough to provide herself with the most basic means of survival. Sooner or later the human body gives in to the abuse it has absorbed and dies. I could not understand how allowing a defenseless person to die on the street could be defined as freedom. Freedom to die under those conditions seems a contradiction in terms.

That night the temperature dipped below thirty-two degrees. Only days before, the mayor had issued a regulation ordering the police to pick homeless people off the street and take them to city shelters, involuntarily if necessary, when the temperature went below the freezing point. Hannah was picked up, against her will. At least she would not freeze to death. The next day she was out on the street again. The temperature had climbed to thirty-three degrees.

◆

Christmas was only a week away. New York City bustled with shoppers, twinkling lights, holiday festivities. The contrast between the energy flowing around us in the city and the heavy despair in the shelter and day program seemed more severe. I did not want to be there. I felt an insidious depression and I feared Joan and Vicki did, too. I knew I was not supporting them enough. I felt badly about it, but I did not seem to have anything left in me to give them. The constant flow of people, the difficulties in helping people find homes, the Hannahs left out in the cold; the overwork, the underpay, the personal pressures in our own lives— it was getting to us, and we could not even be sure we would not be working on Christmas day. I had lined up volunteers to provide Christmas dinner at the shelter, which was to remain open all day. One of Paul's executive assistants was to come in, as she did not celebrate Christmas. But now Paul said we would not know if that was definite until Christmas Eve afternoon, and if not, one of us had to come in. I felt guilty for resisting this so strongly, but my desire to be with my family and Dennis, celebrating the holiday as we traditionally did, prevailed. Christmas—time of joy, time of renewal. I felt my father's death anew, and I felt the suffering all around me. I searched for the love inside me, inside us all, that would fan the embers of hope.

It was Friday afternoon, four days before Christmas. The atmosphere in the day program was bleak. Holidays have their way of imposing more pain on people who no longer have homes or family to enjoy and share them with. The volunteers were great in procuring specially selected gifts for each woman. In addition to these special gifts, we had numerous generic gifts such as hats, gloves, and other practical items. We got a menorah for Stacie, who took deep pride in her Jewish heritage. We got a Christmas tree; we arranged for special foods. It all rang a bit tinny: we could go home, they could not.

So on that Friday afternoon I tried to liven up the atmosphere, to cut through the weighty air, by playing some music. Music has always been a source of comfort for me, so I tried to heal some pain with the keyboard. The church basement had a piano in the corner of the room. I played some of my own music, undoubtedly comforting myself more than anyone else. And then Gloria asked me to play some Christmas carols.

Gloria was stubborn, feisty, suffering from arthritis. She got on everyone's nerves. Gloria had her own way of doing things, forged over seventy-five years, and expected everyone else to follow. She had a passion for the opera and would march over to the radio and turn on the classical station, even if someone else was listening to a different station. "Opera is the most beautiful music in the world. What you want to listen to that other junk for?" she would demand. Old-world Italian, she loved to cook and was always puttering around the kitchen at lunchtime, ordering things to be done in a certain way, complaining that we did not use olive oil, and lamenting over the lack of a good cup of strong espresso. Despite her many years, her mind was as sharp as my own. I grew to love Gloria.

So I played some Christmas carols for her, and she surprised me by coming over to the piano and singing along with the music from a little carol booklet that someone had left there. Her voice was off-key and rattling, and her eyes strained to find the words. When we came to "Silent Night" in the booklet, I decided to join Gloria in singing this, my favorite Christmas carol. Gloria was so short that although she was standing next to the piano bench and I was sitting on it, her head was parallel to my own. We got through about half of "Silent Night" when I realized we were doing more than singing.

Gloria began to sing with an even deeper quaver in her voice. I glanced at her face next to mine and saw tears streaming down her cheeks. I was taken aback. Despite prolonged efforts, Gloria would never say how she had come to be homeless, or where she had lived before. I suspected the pain of going into her past and juxtaposing her present situation against happier times was too much for her to bear, and so she survived by shutting out those memories as best she could. But here with a Christmas carol, her chest heaved with the tears as she struggled to choke out the words of the song.

"Gloria, are you all right?" I asked.

"Yes. Play, play."

We finished the song. I had not been able to continue singing. The sight of her crying moved something in me. I was crying myself. I remembered singing the carol with family, college friends, carolers. Jumbled memories of happy times and a song that seemed almost like a childhood lullaby: " . . . all is calm, all is bright . . . Sleep in heavenly peace." Isn't that what we all yearn for? Gloria, the other women, Joan, Vicki, my family, me—we all have our own pain, our own struggles. But we yearn for the same . things deep within our hearts. Calm and peace sometimes seem very far away, almost irretrievable. It seemed very far away that afternoon, yet in Gloria's stoic "Play, play," I saw that cobweb-fine thread of hope still touching her, and its power lifted my heart. She would sing the carol; she would and could still hope. Her spirit was incomparably more brilliant than any amount of lights strung along Park Avenue. We dried our tears and Gloria shuffled off to the kitchen without a word.

What memories did that carol revive for her? Where had she sung it before and with whom? Would she sing it again next year? Would she still be alive? Would I ever sing that carol again without feeling the same sense of universality as I did that afternoon?

Chapter 7

Rooms for Rent

The new year brought new hope as the coalition went to closing on the SRO. Close to one million dollars had been raised between September and the new year, with individual, foundation, and congregation contributions ranging from two dollars to $350,000. The coalition's board had made it happen. They were proud. This was real housing. It was part of a solution.

At the time of closing, there were seven empty rooms in the SRO. These rooms would be the first round of rooms to be renovated. Occupancy would be withheld until the work was completed. The building was about eighty years old and needed a facelift. It looked as if it had not seen fresh paint in years. Cheap, rotting linoleum covered rotting wooden floors, and the electrical and fire alarm systems needed a major overhaul. Part of the contributions had already been earmarked for these renovations, and the coalition hoped that they would be able to make up the balance by applying for government loans.

The coalition became its own nonprofit operating organization, able to hire people and to have its own payroll. They hired an executive director to run the organization, manage the building, and continue fund-raising: we would need ongoing resources to provide services in the building as well as to continue the day program, dinner program, and soup kitchens. Some of the board members asked me if I wanted to apply for the position, but I felt that I needed more experience working directly with the women and that I could make more improvements in the shelter. I felt strongly that a person could be a good administrator only if she had worked closely with the people she was ultimately hired to serve. Otherwise, decisions could be made that did not correlate with the reality of the people. I was twenty-six years old, and I felt that I still had a lot to learn. I was somewhat disappointed when a woman just a little older than I, with minimal direct experience working with homeless people, was hired. However, she did have considerable administrative experience and seemed very enthusiastic about the job. I looked forward to working together, and was ecstatic about the building.

I felt as if a huge boulder had been rolled off the road. Now we had something tangible to offer the women—affordable housing—a reason for them to believe it made sense to keep trying. The offering was meager—only a room, no cooking facilities, and a shared bathroom—but it was something. At this point, I felt that all the efforts involved in obtaining the SRO had been worthwhile if for only two people: Jackie and her mother, Margaret.

Much had happened since that August day when Margaret returned from the psychiatric hospital. Joan, Vicki, and I had learned about Jackie and Margaret's past, tried to help them plan for the future, and listened to their anger at their current situation. Margaret had lived with her husband and Jackie in a modest Bronx apartment for close to twenty years, after living in other blue-collar neighborhoods in the city during her first several years of marriage. Her husband had been the backbone of the family, holding down a variety of blue-collar jobs and tempering Margaret's erratic personality. Jackie had been hit by a car when she was eleven years old and still suffered, on occasion, from resultant physical disabilities. Coupled with these ailments was a psychological problem that began when she was caught in a burning building as a child. Jackie escaped the fire, but the fear had left its scar: she was inordinately afraid of small, closed places where she felt she might get "trapped." Jackie had held sporadic cashier jobs throughout her adult life but was presently on disability insurance. When Jackie's father died from cancer four years ago, their main source of income disappeared and their family stability died as well.

Three years later, Jackie and Margaret decided to live on the streets. The decision to leave their apartment was based on financial constraints and fear. Margaret's husband's life insurance policy paid for little more than his funeral expenses. A combination of a small monthly pension, a welfare allotment, and Jackie's disability benefits covered the rent, leaving them just a few dollars per month for food, electricity, the telephone, and other expenses. Coupled with these financial difficulties was their belief that they could not continue to live in the same building as their neighbor, Brenda. Brenda lived on the floor below them and had gotten into frequent brawls with Margaret over the past few years, some leading to fistfights. Brenda may have had some psychological problems of her own which fueled Margaret's volatility and resulted in havoc. They had called the police to complain about each other more than once, and the landlord had threatened to throw Margaret and Jackie out if there was any more trouble. Margaret and Jackie suspected that the landlord was somehow prompting Brenda to instigate trouble so that he would have cause to evict them and then rent their apartment at a higher price, but they had no way of proving it.

Fearing Brenda and fearing eviction, they left the apartment rather than risk another confrontation. They did, however, continue to pay their rent each month in the hope that Brenda would eventually move out, allowing them to move back in without fear. They also knew that soon they would be getting a little more money each month: when Margaret turned sixty-two, she would become eligible for Social Security benefits.

After leaving their apartment, they had lived in Central Park for one year, along with their cat, Danny, until someone told them about the newly opened shelter at the settlement house. They had been afraid to go to the city shelters.

Margaret and Jackie had been living at the shelter for about eighteen months when I first met Margaret after her hospital stay in August. At that point, she had already turned sixty-two and was receiving Social Security checks. Her volatile personality had also been stabilized, to put it mildly. These conditions made a move back to the apartment a feasible plan of action, and one I had promised to help Margaret with during her limited shelter stay. But moving someone out of the shelter was rarely a simple matter—this was no exception. A host of minor problems took several weeks to resolve. Margaret no longer had the key to the front door of her apartment building or the mailbox key; Con Ed had long since turned off the electricity, which would not be turned back on until a substantial back bill was paid; a broken boxspring was the only piece of furniture in the apartment that had not been sold; and there was no refrigeration. On top of that, Margaret's money was being controlled by Danny's veterinarian.

When Margaret and Jackie first came to the shelter, Margaret was quite irrational. The previous shelter director thought Margaret was incapable of handling her own money and had initiated a process with the Department of Social Services office to establish that Margaret was incompetent and to appoint a representative payee for her. A representative payee manages a person's finances, paying necessary bills and giving the person an allowance as deemed suitable. Unless a friend or relative agrees to act as a representative payee, a stranger is appointed by the office. Jackie had been opposed to this action from the start, fearing bureaucratic snags with her mother's money and more complications in their already complicated lives, but the director had prevailed.

When the director blocked Jackie's attempts to be the representative payee, Jackie, trying to avoid the appointment of a stranger, reluctantly asked Danny's veterinarian—the only person she had to rely on at the time— if he would accept this responsibility. He had agreed to assume this role, but after a year and a half of the complications involved with getting money to Margaret in a timely fashion and keeping track of all expenditures, he was fed up with it and wanted to relinquish the responsibility. His office and home were in the Bronx while the shelter was in Manhattan. The arrangement, if it made any sense at all to begin with, made less sense as time dragged on. Since neither Jackie, Margaret, nor I saw any reason why Jackie should not be the representative payee, we went through the process to have her approved as the payee and the responsibility officially transferred to her.

Jackie was not planning to move back to the Bronx with her mother, having begun to recognize the rather unhealthy control her mother had exerted over her life. Margaret had been feeding Jackie's fears and insecurities while creating a relationship of total dependency on Jackie. This noose was pulled whenever Jackie showed interest in growing into an independent adult, behaviors which might threaten Margaret's self-interest in keeping Jackie by her side as much as possible. Jackie had decided she was going to make a life for herself at long last. She was thirty-five years old. Barely literate, fearful of closed places (which precluded the use of an elevator, a serious impediment to considering many jobs), and suffering from stomach ailments exacerbated by her heavy weight, Jackie worked against the odds towards the day when she could find employment again. At a counseling center that ran special therapy sessions for phobics, Jackie worked hard on ridding herself of the phobia that had, in part, helped keep her in their apartment for prolonged periods, where she felt in control of her environment. So when we made plans to move Margaret back to the apartment, there was a mutual understanding that Jackie would be a support for her mother but would not give up her life for her.

Margaret did not want to accept these terms, although she had halfheartedly allowed us to work on moving her back to her apartment, according to the agreement of which she had been accepted into the shelter. I had fought with the landlord to get Margaret a new set of keys. It was clear from our conversations that he did not want Margaret back. We negotiated with Con Ed to devise a payment plan for the back bill. Vicki's parents happened to be moving out of their Bronx home into a smaller apartment and offered to give Margaret two single beds and a couch. Vicki transported these to Margaret's apartment in a borrowed station wagon and hauled them up the twisting staircase with a friend. A foundation that gave small grants for special needs donated money to buy Margaret a half-sized refrigerator. Margaret decided not to incur the expense of a telephone after she and Jackie spoke to the elderly woman who lived in the apartment across the hall. This woman agreed to accept phone calls for Margaret.

With the physical aspects of the apartment provided for, we had to work on the internal supports. Because Margaret had been hospitalized and was mentally disabled, she was entitled to receive a few hours of daily home health aide services through Medicaid. Arrangements were made for an aide to spend three hours a day at Margaret's apartment to do such tasks as grocery shopping, light housecleaning, food preparation, etc. That took care of Margaret's daytime needs, but another arrangement was needed to attend to her fear of sleeping alone in the apartment at night. A young college girl, Laura, had begun volunteering after befriending Margaret on the street some time ago. She had recently been thrown out of her home by her mother's new boyfriend. After getting Margaret's approval, I suggested to Laura that she move in with Margaret. Laura gladly accepted the offer of free rent in exchange for keeping Margaret company in the evenings and contributing to food and other ancillary expenses. We had Margaret's medical and psychiatric records transferred from her present outpatient clinic to one only two blocks from her apartment. Connecting her with this outpatient treatment center would help to insure that Margaret would remain in a stable albeit seemingly deadened mental state.

Yet, with everything in place, Margaret still did not want to go. "I want to stay in the shelter," she would say. Of course it was not the shelter but Jackie, she did not want to leave.

"You can't, Margaret. You have a place to go. You're paying rent on it. You should live in it. Jackie won't be far away. Give it a chance," I would tell her.

"I want to stay in the shelter."

The day after Margaret left the shelter, I received a panicky phone call. "Lisa, I'm out on the street. The aide never showed up and I have nothing to eat." Why did something always have to go wrong? We could check and double-check, yet something always seemed to be beyond our control.

I called the home health aide office and got the usual type of reply. "I don't know. She should have been there. Everything was in order. I don't know what went wrong, but we'll make sure she is there tomorrow." Thanks. What was I supposed to do about a scared, lonely lady who had no food and was on a street corner waiting for me to call her back on the pay phone today? Fortunately, I was able to reach Laura before she left school to go to work, and she agreed to stop back at the apartment, check on Margaret, and bring some food. The food was really not such an emergency; Margaret had the money to buy food for herself if she needed. The real issue was that she was scared, and she would rather use the lack of food as an excuse to come back to the shelter where she felt safe, where she had Jackie.

When I called her back to tell her Laura was bringing food, she begged to come back to the shelter.

"I don't want to stay here in the Bronx. The aide won't come. I told you she wouldn't come. Let me come back," she pleaded.

"I can't. You'll be all right. You lived in that apartment for a long time, it's your home. You just have to get used to it again. You have plenty of help now," I said, trying to distance myself emotionally from her entreaties on the other end of the line. Her expressions were still blank, as they had been ever since she was hospitalized, but the intensity of the appeals came through loud and clear. It was very difficult to have to tell her repeatedly that she could not come back, even though I believed that this plan was the only one that made sense.

During her first week at the apartment, Margaret called me every couple of days, frantically asking me to let her come back. I continued to say no, hoping that with time she would adjust to living in the apartment without Jackie.

A few weeks went by, and then another call.

"Lisa, I'm at the phone booth. You have to let me back. I have urine all over me. I can't live here."

"What do you mean, you have urine all over you? Why?" I asked.

"I want to come back," she said flatly.

"You can't."

I called the aide. I called the clinic. What was going on? Why was she not using the bathroom? Was she sick? A trip with Jackie to a clinic revealed no physical cause for incontinence. Two more weeks of the same. Jackie took her to a local hospital emergency room, and, again, no physical reason was found. I started to get mad. We had done everything we could for this woman. Why was she creating this problem? Who was she trying to manipulate with this tactic? Jackie took her to another hospital emergency room at a Manhattan hospital. She had cancer.

My God. Why had I doubted her? Because she had been homeless? Because she was "crazy"? Had I fallen prey to the insanity of those "sane" people who believe that homeless people revel in urinating on the street? Cancer. It seemed impossible that one person could have so much bad luck.

The tumor in her bladder had been causing the incontinence. Because of the prospective complications due to her age and the location and size of the tumor, the doctors decided it was a 50/50 proposition whether to operate or not. If they did not operate, the cancer could spread and eventually kill Margaret; if they did, she could die from the operation. The hospital did a psychiatric evaluation on Margaret and, finding her to be competent, allowed her to choose whether or not to have the operation. She chose not to have it. After a few weeks in the hospital to stabilize her condition as best as was possible, she was released.

An elderly volunteer, Elsie, who often suffered from health problems herself, offered to temporarily share her Manhattan apartment with Margaret so she could be close to the hospital clinic for her checkups. This also made it more convenient for Jackie to visit frequently and to accompany her to the doctor. Elsie was quite generous to offer her home in this way, yet she did it in a simple, unselfconscious way, as if loving another human being was the most natural expression of all.

Margaret and Jackie decided that the Bronx apartment was too much to handle now that Margaret was ill. Jackie wanted her to be near the Manhattan hospital that was treating her mother, and was concerned that if the cancer spread, Margaret might need more intensive supportive services. Since the coalition would have on-site services at the SRO, and Jackie could be near her to provide help, as was her desire, Margaret was put on the list for a room. So after all the work of setting up the apartment, Margaret finally terminated the lease. A volunteer, Brian, who ran a music appreciation group at the day program, offered to help me move Margaret's things temporarily to Elsie's apartment. We brought the donated refrigerator to the SRO so that it could eventually be used by the residents in a common room.

◆

During this interim period, Jackie had also managed to get out of the shelter. She was living a few blocks away from the shelter with a volunteer who took a particular interest in her. The agreement was that Jackie could live there until the SRO was ready to take new tenants, or until another housing option became available. It was by all means temporary. Mrs. Fox, the volunteer, was a middle-aged woman with a family that was grown and on their own, leaving several of the rooms in her attractive brownstone empty. (The brownstone was probably worth well over a million dollars.) Mrs. Fox had agreed to let Jackie live in a first-floor room that had its own entrance and bath. They would share the kitchen, also located on the first floor. In exchange for the room, Jackie had agreed to do light housekeeping and to feed and change the litter box for Mrs. Fox's two cats. The arrangement was working out well but for the fact that Mrs. Fox had not been looking for a permanent boarder, and time continued to stretch lazily as Jackie searched for a permanent home.

Jackie was searching for an apartment for herself in every way imaginable. She had applied for public housing, but with about 200,000 people on the waiting list for federally subsidized, low-rent housing, and estimates of a wait up to eighteen years, this was obviously not an immediate solution. Applying for public housing was an exercise many people in these circumstances went through. Although the exercise seemed futile, there was little else out there even to hope for: one had to try to do something, apply for something, or the feeling of futility in looking for affordable housing might become engulfing. Section 8 certificates were another means to low-income housing, also with long waiting lists. Section 8 certificates were given sparingly to persons whose income fell below a certain level. The person with a certificate was responsible for finding his or her own apartment. Once found, the occupant would pay a third of his or her income towards the rent; the government would pay the balance, provided the rent was low enough to fall within eligibility guidelines. Jackie had applied for a certificate two years earlier and was notified that her number had come up.

Jackie was jubilant when she got her certificate, only to be angered and dismayed to find that most landlords reject Section 8 certificate-holders because they are viewed as problematic, since the landlord then has to deal with the government and its bureaucracy to collect the rent. In addition, finding an apartment that had an acceptable rent according to Section 8 guidelines was like finding a parking space in midtown Manhattan on a weekday in the rain. Jackie's certificate expired before she could locate an apartment, so she continued to check newspaper ads for affordable rental units and any housing that had units set aside for the disabled.

People living outside New York City might think that she did not look hard enough; people who have themselves looked for an apartment in New York City know better. I was one of them, and it was quite an education. Before Vivian moved to New York City, another girlfriend and I had looked for an apartment together. We were willing to spend about half of our take-home pay on rent, equivalent to $1,000 a month for a one-bedroom apartment—a sum several times the amount that welfare or disability benefits would pay. Real estate brokers charged fifteen percent of the year's rent as their fee and insisted that it was impossible to find such a "cheap" apartment. They also informed us that since we did not have a combined salary of at least $50,000, we had to have the lease signed by a family member who did, or we would not even be considered as prospective tenants.

Trying to avoid the brokers, we poured over the classified section of every newspaper that ran apartment listings. It was like a race to see who would get to the leaseholder or landlord first, and we never seemed to be the winners. In any case, the person handing over the lease usually charged an enormous "fixture fee," roughly equivalent to what a broker would have charged. We rejoiced when it appeared that we had finally been the first to reach a landlord with an apartment in our price range, handing the landlord a $950 check for a security deposit in exchange for a standard lease, no fixture fee. We felt acute rage when the landlord barred us from moving in, and we realized we must have been one set of many who had been "rented" that same apartment. Taking him through the court process took months: he hired a lawyer, we did not, and we only got half of our money back in the end. This was my personal initiation into the housing system in New York City.

My girlfriend was so disgusted that she decided to move to Westchester instead. Considering I was starting out with the advantage of making almost four times as much as someone at the poverty level, it was painfully clear why so many people were doomed to languish in "emergency" shelters. A person living on a fixed income with no savings, worn clothing, and no financially comfortable friends or relatives had very little chance of finding an affordable apartment.

Jackie called every SRO she could find. The response was invariable: no rooms. SROs used to be a ready housing resource for poor people before city-promoted tax incentives enticed developers to convert these buildings into luxury units, or simply to demolish them towards the same end. This policy was largely responsible for the loss of over 100,000 SRO units in New York City within a decade. Most remaining SROs are in terrible condition, since the landlords know that they can rent out all their rooms whether or not they maintain the building. The demand for SRO rooms so overwhelms the supply that landlords can get away with providing poor heat (or none at all), unsanitary living conditions with mice, rat, and roach infestations, crumbling walls, faulty plumbing, and poor security. Some SROs have hot-plate cooking facilities and sinks in individual rooms; some do not. The demand for these remaining rooms grows as the stock of affordable housing continues to shrink.

So Jackie, luckier than most because she had managed to get out of the shelter, if only temporarily, continued to live with Mrs. Fox while waiting for the coalition to renovate the vacant rooms in their SRO. January turned into February, turned into March, and Tracy, the new executive director kept saying "soon." We had not expected the work to take so long.

During this stage of limbo, it became more burdensome for Jackie to handle Margaret's finances. Jackie was caring for Mrs. Fox's cats and doing other cat-sitting jobs, cleaning Mrs. Fox's house, going to her therapy group, visiting her mother and taking her to doctor's appointments, and looking for housing. Handling Margaret's money was one more responsibility, and one that no longer seemed necessary. Margaret had been maintaining her mental stability since I met her in August. She was still lethargic with respect to her outward expressions but was otherwise totally coherent and rational. She wanted control of her own money, and it seemed quite reasonable that she should have it. If the hospital psychiatrist had deemed Margaret competent enough to decide whether or not to elect surgery, she could certainly decide whether the small amount of Social Security and pension money she received each month should be spent for new shoes, extra bread, and other small necessities. We began investigating how she could regain control, a process more laborious than I had ever imagined.

Not having the vaguest notion about the legal motions necessary to reverse this payeeship, I called the Legal Aid Society, which provides government-supported legal services for the poor. I was shunted from one office call to another, each person telling me Margaret was in a different jurisdiction than the one they served. I backtracked, trying to get the same answer twice out of somebody, hoping I would eventually get someone who really knew what office should handle Margaret's geographic area. When I finally reached that office, I was told that Margaret had to come in person for information, and that they could not dispense information over the telephone. I asked if I could set up an appointment for her, and was told that she just had to go to the office and wait her turn, which usually took several hours. Explaining that she was elderly and was being treated for cancer did no good. Those were the rules.

Jackie took Margaret to the office that week. They came back weary and angry. After waiting for hours, they were told that they did not provide legal assistance in such cases because they were too overloaded, and were directed to contact the county clerk to initiate the legal process and to plead their case in court. Margaret might have been able to handle her own money, but to have expected her to represent herself in an intimidating court atmosphere was a bit much. I was infuriated and felt badly for making them waste their time going there. I was also frustrated by the difficulties involved in getting the simple information that would give us a starting point for working on the problem.

I called the county clerk who had been involved with the initial proceedings involving the veterinarian to inquire about how Margaret could become her own payee again. He was nasty and curt, informing me that Jackie could come to the office with certain documentation if we wanted to avoid going to court. This was obviously preferable, so we set up an appointment and Jackie made the trip to his Bronx office. She came back in a somewhat hysterical state later that day to tell me she had never met with the clerk because his office was on the second floor of the building, she had been too scared to go up in the elevator, and the stairwell had been locked. She went to the corner pay phone and spoke to his secretary, who refused to come down and open the stairwell door. I called the clerk and was informed in a dry manner that he knew of no phone call, only that she had never shown up and that he had already filed the papers that would make a court hearing necessary. It was all so infuriating.

No longer having any recourse, we gathered information and documentation and rehearsed what we would say in front of the judge. The case was on the calendar within a few weeks.

Mrs. Fox offered to go with us for moral support for Margaret, who was nervous about the proceeding. It was a freezing morning when all of us assembled at her house to head to the Bronx courthouse together. Buses were running behind schedule as they crushed the snow and ice under their wheels. I was afraid we would be late, but we made it to the courthouse steps with ten minutes to spare. Once inside, I asked where Courtroom B was and found it was on the fourth floor. Jackie began to panic.

"I can't go," Jackie blurted nervously. "I'm scared of elevators. I can't go. Sorry Mom, I just can't do it."

"You can walk up the stairs," Mrs. Fox said. "Now Jackie, don't start this."

"I can't go! I can't go!" Jackie exclaimed. We had walked over to the stairwell door. "What if it's locked on top? What if it locks behind us? What if we get trapped?!" She was hysterical.

I had read about phobic reactions and worked with phobics on a psychiatric ward, but this was the first time I was witnessing a full-blown phobic attack. I had not realized the extent of the reaction before. Jackie was completely frantic, losing control of herself, breathing rapidly, sweating.

"Now Jackie, you can do it if you really want to," Mrs. Fox cajoled. She ran up the stairs, coming back down with the news that the door was unlocked. "Why don't you give it a try?" she asked sweetly.

"Excuse me, Mrs. Fox," I said. "Do you think you could wait for us with Margaret in the courtroom? I'd like to talk to Jackie alone." Nice as Mrs. Fox was, I felt she was being too soft on Jackie, too maternal. We had not come this far to lose the case because we could not get up the stairs. I was going to get Jackie up there, end of story.

"I'm sorry, Lisa," Jackie whined, "I just can't do it."

Jackie's fear was real, and she was feeding into that fear with her whole being.

"Jackie, control yourself," I said sharply. "Stop talking and listen. We came a long way to get this far. If you don't want to deal with this money nonsense any more, you'll have to get up those stairs."

"I can't, Lisa. I can't. I have a phobia."

"Stop. I did not come here to hear this. Now the door is unlocked on top and it's unlocked here. Move! I'll be right behind you."

Jackie started up the first step, turning and beginning to whine and back down.

"Go, Jackie. Take one step at a time. Don't stop and don't turn around," I said. I suddenly felt as if I were viewing Hitchcock's final scene in *Vertigo*, with Jackie taking the James Stewart role.

Four flights and Jackie's two hundred plus pounds was no jaunt. We went slowly, but we went. Jackie was still experiencing extreme anxiety along the way, but it was controlled; she was coping with it. When we got to the top and out the door, we were both thrilled.

"You did it! I knew you could. Little by little you'll learn to overcome it—just don't give in to the fear," I said.

"I made it all right," Jackie said with a mixture of relief and pride. "I hope they didn't call Mama's name yet."

We walked into the courtroom as the judge read through the list of names on the roster. The room was of rich wood, the judge imposing. The room and everyone in it looked formal. I had played the game. I was wearing a dark gray suit and white shirt, and had pulled my hair back in a stern bun. So far it had worked. The man at the inspection desk in the lobby had initially let me by, saying "Lawyer, right?" When I said no, he stopped me and checked for weapons. I had worn the requisite costume to look as powerful as I could since I certainly was not feeling powerful. That judge would decide if Margaret was to be treated as mentally stable or not. So much would depend on how we said what we did and how we were perceived by the court.

I presented the case to the judge, who then asked Margaret to take the stand and explain how much money she got each month and what her average monthly living expenses were. She presented herself very well, and after a few more questions, the whole thing was over. The judge decided Margaret could handle her own finances on the condition that the coalition continue to provide social work services and monitoring during the following three months. I was required to send a report after that time period to vouch for Margaret's ability to handle the money. If she had done well, which I had no doubt she would, the decision would remain. Otherwise, he would reverse it. I was ecstatic. We had won!

Margaret and Jackie were nonchalant. I was mystified at first. "Yeah, we won. But we wouldn't have been in this mess in the first place if the old shelter director hadn't started this legal nonsense. I knew it was bad news from the start. Look at all the trips we had to make these past two years to the clerk, Danny's vet, the courthouse! It makes me sick," Jackie said angrily. I understood her anger at being forced into dealing with so much bureaucracy over what seemed like an enormous exercise in futility, over a very small amount of money. Perhaps it had made sense to the former director, but it did not seem to make much sense in hindsight. At any rate, I was happy that at least one hurdle had been overcome. From Jackie's perspective—two years in the shelter, little financial resources, few prospects of permanent housing, and a mother with cancer—such a gain was small consolation.

◆

Renovation work had snowballed at the SRO. When the workers tried to patch the cracks in the walls of the vacant rooms, the plaster came crumbling down, leaving big sections of the walls completely bare. The work was going to take even longer than expected. It was clear now that most of the rooms needed to have the walls entirely replaced. The floors were being worked on too. So Margaret and Jackie continued waiting, along with several of the other women slated for the first vacant rooms.

◆

As March came to a close, I said goodbye to my job at the shelter. After deciding not to apply for the executive director position, in part so that I could continue to work at the shelter and gather more experience there, I was rather shocked when Tracy told me one day in a matter-of-fact way that my services were no longer needed at the shelter. Apparently, she and Paul had decided that now that the coalition was its own operating organization, the arrangement with the settlement house would no longer work. They agreed that the settlement house agency would take over the operation of the shelter. Specifically, this meant that the agency would pay for all shelter costs, including the salary given to the shelter director, who would then be settlement house agency staff. The coalition would continue to staff the day program, provide social services to the residents at the SRO, and continue to coordinate the soup kitchens and dinner program.

I felt betrayed. I had put my heart into that shelter. I had worked hard to make it better. I had plans for more improvements in service, and I had grown to care a great deal about those women. Maria intervened on my behalf, and after some discussion I was given the option of applying for the shelter director position or remaining with the coalition as program director. It was a hard decision. I felt that the shelter was my child: I had nurtured it, and it had given expression to my maternal instincts to shelter and make safe people I cared about. I had not realized how much it had become a part of me until I was faced with giving it up. I was startled by this realization. I had fought with that underlying current of "mothering" the women that I had felt from the start, and yet it had crept in unawares. I liked feeling I was helping to take care of these women. When I realized that, I realized it was time to go; it had gotten too cozy. It was not good to feel self-satisfied for running a shelter that was a little cleaner, a little more organized or friendly. It was too easy to forget that, decent shelter or not, we must never be self-satisfied for merely helping people get a temporary roof over their heads. When we institutionalize homelessness, we have lost the vision of a humane society.

I was also eager to see the women move into the SRO and to be a part of that process. I wanted to see the circle close. One consolation of leaving the shelter was that I would no longer need to work late nights or stay overnight there. This was particularly attractive to me now, because Dennis had just transferred to the New York City office of his firm and had moved into the city two weeks before. I began to adjust to the idea of having a more "normal" lifestyle, seeing Dennis and friends in the evenings, maybe taking a music class. Still, I would miss the challenge. I would be one more step removed from the women's day-to-day reality. It took awhile to adjust from the chaotic, noisy, crowded world of almost daily crises to a calmer existence. Not deciding who gets a bed, not throwing people out, not dealing with basic needs like bathing, not turning people away — all these responsibilities fell away from me. But the machine would churn on, with someone else to pull the levers.

Chapter 8

Just Get a Job!

◆

Leaving the shelter meant I no longer had office space. Until office space was created at the SRO, I used the day program as my base. It was a nice opportunity to offer more support to Joan, who had been carrying the work of the day program almost single-handedly, but it was aggravating for both of us to share the limited staff space. The staff space consisted of use of the top of the choir director's desk; the drawers were off limits. The desk sat in a corner of the unpartitioned church basement. A telephone on the desk had to be shared among Joan, me, and all of the women at the program who might need to call the Department of Social Services, doctors, landlords, employment agencies, and so on. The locked entrance door, located across the room atop a long, winding staircase, could only be answered by a staffperson. This was very inconvenient because unless both of us were at the day program, it inevitably meant leaving someone waiting while a phone call was finished, or dropping the phone and running up and down the long flight of stairs. These were the conditions originally given us by the minister in order to use the space. Having no other offers, we had accepted gladly. As I spent more time at the day program and realized just how difficult the lack of privacy and office materials made it to do any productive casework, I marveled at Joan's good nature. I never heard her complain.

Joan and I both had to adjust to losing Vicki. The settlement house agency started a street outreach program in April and Vicki had taken one of the positions on the outreach team. Her job was to work with homeless people who were living on the streets in the neighborhood, to help them avail themselves of shelter and other supports. It was a good move for Vicki, but we missed the daily contact with her.

The absence of my shelter responsibilities allowed me to devote more time to tasks that had been on the back burner. One of these was organizing volunteer training, which I had never gotten around to doing on a formal basis. Previously, I had spent thirty to sixty minutes with each new volunteer, explaining the programs, how to fit in, and giving a cursory background on homelessness and what to expect at the shelter. I had had ideas for running a more structured training program for groups of volunteers, and now I finally had the time to implement them. I decided to hold monthly seminars, with a speaker presenting lecture material for one hour followed by an hour of discussion. Each seminar was designed to cover a different aspect of homelessness. The first one was an overview, and I decided I would present this lecture myself, lining up guest lecturers for the rest. Flyers advertising the seminar were sent to all the volunteers, and the church hosting the session advertised the seminar outside the parish hall. About forty-five people came to the first seminar, including Jean and Lily, who had seen the church posting and decided to come. At first I was surprised, but then I realized the irony of the situation. They had more reason than anyone else to be there and to try to make any sense of their predicament.

After I gave my talk, I asked a preselected group of volunteers to describe to the group what type of work they had been doing at the program so new volunteers could get an idea of the variety of different ways they might be of service. Chandler spoke about her role as a job counsultant. Chandler had been coming to the day program every Monday morning since the program's inception eight months earlier. She spent time with women who were seeking employment, counseling them on an individual basis regarding the field they were most suited for, how to market themselves, and general job search tactics. Jean came to see her religiously. She now sat in the audience, listening attentively. As Chandler described her efforts, I wondered if Jean felt bitter or angry. Did she think her own efforts at finding employment had been another cruel joke played by society against her?

It had taken months for Chandler to help Jean believe that she could do anything worthy of financial reimbursement. Jean had spent her entire life caring for her parents. She had worked very hard, but she had never earned a paycheck. In order to find housing, Jean knew she would have to find a paying job, because it was impossible to find any place to live on Lily's extremely low Social Security check. (Applying for welfare was something Jean would not consider in her wildest dreams.) The coalition's SRO was not a possibility for Jean and Lily because the law allowed only one person per room in an SRO, and Jean felt they needed to be in the same room. Lily often began to roll off the bed in the middle of the night, and Jean feared she might hurt herself and that she was too frail in general to be left alone.

Making the transition from family caregiver to family caregiver *and* wage earner was not easy. Jean wanted to work, yet she was not about to apply for nine-to-five jobs and leave her eighty-five-year-old, half-blind mother to fend for herself during the day. A night job was not possible either, because if Jean was to work at night she would have no way of getting any sleep; the shelter was closed from 7 A.M. until 10 P.M. Being middle-aged with no employment experience was quite a hurdle as well. Finally, after prolonged discussions, Jean decided that a housekeeping job was the solution. After all, Jean had been a housekeeper and nursemaid her whole life, only she did not get paid for it. Jean and Chandler proposed that Jean could bring Lily with her on housekeeping jobs and might even be able to get a live-in position.

Situation-wanted ads were put up on all the local church bulletin boards as well as in several newspapers and local publications. Ideally, Jean hoped to find an elderly lady who lived alone and needed housekeeping services, and who had an extra room where she and Lily could live. However, Jean was more than willing to take day or half-day work, anything to get started and begin to save money. Several people responded to the ads, which led to several interviews; each interview brought the same response. They liked Jean, but would not hire her without work references. Her mother was her only work-related reference, and that was not good enough. So many disappointments. I wondered how she got up the courage to keep trying.

Jean sat in the back of the room listening to me wrap up the seminar by asking the volunteers to reach out and do more. And my conscience began to tickle. My roommate, Vivian, had been volunteering with a church-based group that ran a shelter for men; she had thought about establishing a job bank to help homeless people find employment opportunities. Vivian had asked me if any of the women involved with the coalition were seeking employment, and I had told her about Jean. They met, and Vivian then asked me if, at her own expense, she could hire Jean to clean our apartment every other week. The real purpose of this was not because Vivian necessarily wanted housekeeping services, but that she then could serve as a bona fide reference for Jean.

I had reacted with a strong no. Social workers are repetitiously trained to be "professional," to keep an emotional distance, not to get too involved with the client. The prospect of having Jean clean our apartment was a little too close for comfort. If there were problems, the trust Jean had developed with the staff could be jeopardized, impeding her future progress on other issues. That aside, my imagination ran wild. What if Lily had a heart attack in our apartment while Jean was cleaning? I could see the headlines: "Elderly homeless lady dies while daughter cleans program director's apartment." What if she fell? I imagined there could be all sorts of negative personal implications from Vivian's efforts to do something nice for them. I told her to forget the idea.

But days later, looking at Jean sitting in the seminar trying to make some sense out of her predicament, I realized I was playing it safe for selfish reasons more than out of a concern for her. There were ways I could ensure our relationship would stay the same. The "professional" line was one I never really bought to begin with, although I was aware that Tracy felt rather strongly to the contrary. When I got home that night, I told Vivian to hire Jean if she wanted to, but not to let Jean know I was her roommate, so that if something went wrong with their working relationship or the job it would not jeopardize our relationship. Joan and I were working with Jean and Lily on other problems, such as housing and a bureaucratic problem with Lily's Social Security checks, which I did not want this new arrangement to disturb. My "room" consisted of an area of the living room partitioned by a rice-paper screen, which Vivian would instruct Jean not to clean. The first day Jean came to our apartment, she spent four hours cleaning the kitchen. The kitchen was five by seven feet; there simply was not that much to clean. Vivian spent considerable time with her during the following few days explaining that people generally do not expect the grout between the tile to come up sparkling white in old apartment buildings, nor do they expect all the silverware to be polished. Jean was so incredibly meticulous that cleaning an apartment according to her standards would take several days work. Vivian helped her prioritize tasks in accordance with what most people would be willing to pay, since people had expectations of what should be done if they were paying a day or half-day rate. Jean huffed about American standards not being up to European, but reluctantly went along with Vivian's suggestions.

After a few more days in our apartment, Vivian felt secure that Jean would do a great job in anyone's home. She began calling her Harvard Business School cohorts, who were likely to hire housekeepers, to ask if they needed such services. Within a week, Vivian found one friend who needed services for a half day every other week, and a married couple who needed a full day once a week. All were thrilled with Jean, finding her to be incredibly conscientious and trustworthy, and no one minded in the least that Lily accompanied her. Jean, never one to be outwardly emotional, did seem to be pleased in her own way. The couple paid her fifty dollars for the day. With the other half day every other week, she was already earning more than what her mother received from Social Security. Between their two incomes, Jean and Lily now had a chance of getting into a building opening downtown.

This building project was similar to the SRO project undertaken by the coalition. The SRO building had been purchased by a non-profit organization formed expressly for the purpose of renting rooms to homeless people. It was now being renovated. Most of the rooms in the building shared bathroom and kitchen facilities on the hall, but there were also three spacious studio apartments with private kitchens and baths in the building. The studios were being reserved for couples. The building management had in mind married couples, but when I explained Jean and Lily's situation, they said they would consider their application for one of the studios. The SRO was a Section 8 building, which meant that the rent for each room could not exceed one-third of the occupants' combined income. We held our breath.

I thanked God that nonprofit organizations were getting into housing. Without the few new nonprofit SROs (this downtown project, the coalition's SRO, and one uptown), there would be little tangible hope, since there were long waiting lists at the few existent nonprofit SROs, and the government was not adequately responding to the emergency. Some short-term solutions were in place because the court system had forced the city to open more shelters, but a comprehensive long-term strategy to satisfy the needs for low-income housing was not to be found. The city turned its head as it continued to lose more and more low-income dwellings to high-income dwellings, with no mechanism to replace the low-income units that were lost.

Where did the city think poor people were going to go? Perhaps they hoped they would move out, move away. But the numbers! The vast numbers—thousands and thousands of individuals and families who were now homeless. They would not melt away. They could not. There was nowhere for them to go. Areas as scourged as Harlem and the South Bronx offered few places to actually live in because so many buildings had been abandoned or burned; the carcasses were now being purchased by people who speculated that those areas were the next to be gentrified. No, these homeless people would remain as a reminder of what we as a society have become. I wonder why there is so little shame.

So we hoped this eighty-five-year-old, frail immigrant who had lost her husband, a good portion of her eyesight, her home, and way of life, all within the year, would get this studio apartment with her daughter. Lily always had a gentle smile on her lips and was accepting and dignified, walking weakly on Jean's arm. I had to believe it was love—of Jean, of God—that sustained her. I could not imagine what else did.

◆

Through this time of hopeful anticipation, as we waited for these three SROs to finish their respective building renovations and to begin accepting new tenants, we saw some people slip farther away. Suzanne was living in the park again. When the settlement house agency had announced that they had gotten funding to start a neighborhood outreach team, Suzanne's intense feelings about the concept of freedom were aroused. Considering Suzanne's reaction to our treatment of Hannah, it came as no surprise that she thought the outreach team was an infringement on the freedom of people who "chose" to live on the street ("chose" or had no choice?). She said she wanted no part of the shelter once the outreach team started. She kept to her word, moving back to her rock in the park the day the team began.

Joan and I made visits to her in the park once or twice a week, encouraging Suzanne at least to come to the day program or the dinners, where she had finally begun eating over the past few months. Her appetite was not large, and she only ate whatever vegetarian foods were offered, but she ate. She now refused even this, sliding into a severe paranoid state, more confused with each day. Suzanne began to speak of her mother frequently now, and she spoke of a desire to kill herself. The fountains had been turned off in the park due to a drought, so Suzanne had no ready water supply. She would not accept food or drink from Joan, me, or Renee for fear of poisoning. Rats had to be shooed away from a large fish carcass that Suzanne had pulled out of the garbage and then enshrined with flowers next to her on the rock. She cried frequently, scribbling furiously on notebook pads that were already completely covered with illegible writings. She ate grass from the earth to try to keep her body alive. And she had her "freedom."

We could not get her hospitalized. The health team's part-time psychiatrist evaluated her in the park and felt she was not overtly suicidal, so he could not hospitalize her. Suzanne, champion of freedom for street people. Freedom . . . freedom to what? I did not understand Suzanne's concept of freedom. She was not free to live. She was destroying that opportunity while we, as a society, were allowing her the freedom to die, painfully and slowly. Freedom to live makes sense to me; freedom to die does not.

Then one day she was gone. No one knew where she had gone or whether she had died in the night. Joan called the few outreach teams in the city to ask them to look for Suzanne and to let us know if they found her, and Renee called the local hospitals to ascertain whether she had been admitted during the night. Renee took her disappearance very hard. "It's like letting a child die on the street," she said tearfully. "She doesn't know any better." We had all tried so hard. We all felt a loss, and at a loss. All we could do was look forward; looking back was too painful.

◆

As the building renovations progressed, we became more excited about the day when the first shelter guests would move in. Weekly meetings were held at the SRO to promote discussions about what it was going to be like to live there. The purpose of these meetings was to soften the transition from the shelter to the SRO by helping people become acclimated to their new surroundings before the actual move. What was revealed in some of the discussions was fear—fear of leaving the shelter, fear of leaving that familiarity, fear of being "alone" for the first time in a long time. It was very understandable. It had been too long. Shelter life had become an institution, a way of life.

The women getting the first available rooms were those who had been at the shelter the longest and were capable of living independently—financially, physically, and mentally. Mental illness would not preclude acceptance into the building, but it could not interfere with the person's ability to respect other people's rights to privacy, quiet, and cleanliness. Beth, Jackie, Margaret, Gloria, Karen (a relative newcomer), and Stacie were to get six of the rooms, and a homeless man who regularly attended the soup kitchens would get the seventh. Leslie, Jean, and Lily had fortunately been accepted into the downtown SRO and were waiting eagerly for their rooms to be renovated. Stacie was also accepted for a room at the uptown SRO, in the same neighborhood as her methadone clinic. Since that SRO was undergoing a gut renovation, it would take a much longer time for the building to be completed. Stacie would live at the coalition's SRO until the other was ready. The remaining women at the shelter were either not receptive to or unable to live on their own at this point, or were recent shelter arrivals who did not have priority for getting into the first group of available rooms.

The issue of who was to get the available rooms crystallized my growing suspicion that Tracy and I operated on different wavelengths. Although we developed a democratic process to decide who to accept into the SRO, Tracy set most of the ground rules in advance, based on what she thought made sense for the building. I did not agree with some of the ground rules, nor the exactitude with which they were enforced. I had had to argue and plead with her to give Jackie and Stacie rooms. She did not want to accept Jackie because she and her cat, Danny, were a package deal, and Tracy wanted a "no pets" policy. But Jackie and the cat had basically been promised a room by board members for months and months. Danny was very clean and housebroken and had been part of Jackie's life for many years. We simply had to accept her.

As for Stacie, Tracy wanted all drug addicts to have been through a residential drug rehabilitation program before getting a room. Since Stacie still occasionally lapsed into Elevil use, Tracy wanted her to go into a drug program. But getting a homeless, penniless woman a coveted slot in a drug rehabilitation program would take years. Besides, the room was only temporary until the uptown SRO was completed. Tracy finally did agree to accept both Jackie and Stacie, but it had not been easy to convince her. I felt that Tracy had a bureaucratic, rigid way of viewing the world. One had to be flexible working with homeless people. There were too many factors, too many particular individual circumstances that needed to be weighed. Strict rules just did not make sense, to my mind. We disagreed on this fairly sharply, and it fatigued me to feel that I had to be an advocate for the women even within the organization itself. Tracy believed her way was right, I believed my way was. The tension was very unpleasant.

◆

The anticipation I felt for the women moving out of the shelter was keen. Each person had circumstances that made getting out of the shelter seem especially welcome, but I suppose Karen was someone I felt particularly happy for. She had traveled a dismal and lonely road, and in a sense, had to overcome the most disadvantages to be able to live on her own. Karen was mildly retarded.

Karen first came to our day program back in December. A local church had called Joan to ask if they could refer her to our program for shelter and other services. Karen had been sleeping on their steps for over a year, during which time various church personnel had tried to convince her to seek shelter. She had remained intensely noncommunicative, refusing offers of assistance until that week in December. She began to indicate a willingness to go to a shelter, but only if it was part of the church. Since our shelter was sponsored by many religious institutions, they called us.

When Karen showed up at the day program that week, she was incredibly dirty from her time on the street. Her nature was extremely gentle, she was soft-spoken and coherent, yet it became apparent within a few minutes of conversation that something was unusual about Karen: something about her facial features and expressions, something about the simplicity of her speech, something about the childlike innocence that she conveyed, all the more surprising coming from someone who had been living on the streets. The expectation that the world and all those in it are loving and good is usually but a tainted memory by the time someone has reached the age of fifty-five, as Karen had.

There was no doubt that Karen knew pain, but she seemed to experience it with bewilderment. She was not embittered by her suffering; she seemed to know no malice whatsoever. She was a mildly retarded adult trying to exist on her own in a complicated world, a feat that required more skills of her than she inherently possessed.

Karen made dramatic changes within a very short period of time. She was quite happy to bathe regularly at the shelter and gratefully accepted a new set of clothes from the donation closet. She was especially pleased with her "new" secondhand coat. It was a burgundy colored, thickly quilted knee-length coat with a real fur collar of chocolate-brown opossum. When everyone complimented Karen on her appearance, she beamed, practically ready to burst with pride and delight. It took so little to make Karen happy. I often wondered about her mother and what she would have felt if she knew what a turn her daughter's life would take after her death.

Joan, who worked very closely with Karen, was able to piece together a rough sketch of her life. Karen had grown up with her family in Connecticut, spending the last twenty years or so living in the family home with her mother. During her adult years she had worked in two or three clerical positions, holding down each job for many years. Then Karen's mother died. Whether any provisions had been made for this eventuality is not known, but if there were, they fell apart, because Karen described her life after her mother died as one of homelessness. She hitchhiked across the country several times during the two years after her mother's death until she landed and remained in New York City over one year ago. One can only imagine the experiences Karen must have had. Traveling alone, no money, limited mental resources, wrenched from a life of security and love, trusting. Whatever experiences she had were enough to teach her not to let the world in anymore, to withdraw as she had, huddled on the church steps for over a year.

Shortly after Karen joined us, she had a brief hospitalization for a severely infected leg ulcer, swollen to the size of a grapefruit. It was by chance we discovered that she needed medical help. Karen had not complained of any pain and wore pants every day, so we had not seen her leg. It was only after another shelter guest reported seeing the ulcerated leg when Karen was getting into bed that it was brought to our attention. Perhaps such physical hardships had become so commonplace for Karen that she did not consider them to be noteworthy. Perhaps she was simply not aware that she could receive medical attention. At any rate, she was quite happy to have the leg treated and was full of her shy smiles when she came back to the shelter.

Joan worked with Karen on a case plan. Karen was more than willing to try to find ways to make it possible for her to live on her own, but she did not want the plan to include what she considered to be charity. Like many of the women we met, she did not want to accept welfare. However, Karen's mental disability made her eligible for Social Security Income (SSI) payments, which are administered through the Social Security system and seem to carry less of a stigma than welfare, which is administered through the Department of Social Services. Joan convinced Karen that it made sense for her to file for SSI while she was looking for work so that the SSI payments could help her through the interim period between seeking and finding employment. Karen was eager to do office work again, as she had for most of her adult life, and to be able to pay for a room for herself.

Karen's search for part- or full-time clerical work proved fruitless. Even with her experience in filing, there were so many people who were willing to take minimum-wage filing jobs that no employer was willing to hire Karen, whom they perceived had a disadvantage by being mentally slow. Joan tried to find a religious institution that could use office help, but none seemed to have the funds to hire someone with limited capabilities. It was a discouraging process. Joan helped Karen apply for a spot in a workshop program that trained and placed disabled people, but she was put on their long waiting list and told that it would probably be many months before she was accepted. Karen and Joan continued to search, and continued waiting.

Every Friday morning, a professional artist, George, volunteered his time to run an art group for any women at the day program who chose to participate. Sometimes five or six women would join George at his table of colors and paper, sometimes only one or two. Karen was a steady customer. It was a pleasant discovery for Karen to learn that she had innate artistic abilities. Her paintings and drawings reflected her gentle and cheerful nature as soft pastels of flowers or landscapes flowed from her hand. The art class offered Karen an avenue where she could excel, and one could see her become increasingly confident and interactive over the weeks and months. She was still extremely quiet, but she was no longer withdrawn.

So when renovation work on the vacant rooms in the coalition's SRO were finally completed in mid-May, I was glad Karen would be getting a room. It had been a long trip.

◆

Karen adjusted better than the others to her new surroundings. She was happy and proud about having her own place, tacking several of her paintings on the walls of her room to personalize her new environment. She continued coming to the day program to work with Joan and Chandler, the volunteer job counselor, on the job search, as well as for socializing and for lunch. For the other women, the transition from the shelter to an SRO room was not so easy.

Gloria did not accept a room, opting to wait for a room in the downtown SRO where she would have access to a communal kitchen. Although the coalition planned to eventually have a communal room with a kitchenette, it looked like it would be a long way off. The half-sized refrigerator that the volunteer and I had lugged up to a storage room had been brought down to an alleyway in the back of the SRO, at Tracy's request. It rusted after being exposed to the rain, and she had it thrown away. I was angry at this wasted resource and wasted effort, but my point of view seemed to be increasingly overruled by Tracy's.

The room we had saved for Gloria now added another room to one already slotted for a homeless man from one of the coalition's soup kitchens. Although the SRO was for homeless men as well as women, we had initially set aside more rooms for women, since one of the primary purposes of buying the building had been so that the women at the shelter would have an affordable means of getting out. Jackie, Margaret, Beth, and Stacie joined Karen as the coalition's first new tenants.

The largest renovated room was on the third floor, faced the street, and had a large window opening onto a fire escape. It went to Margaret. Since Margaret and Jackie had been at the shelter the longest, the room had been shown to them first. In deference to her mother, Jackie opted for a smaller room three doors down. It had two small windows looking onto an alleyway. The room, like all but the front and back rooms, had no fire escape, although fire escapes outside the hallway windows were easily accessible. Nevertheless, when Jackie tried to sleep there, her phobic reaction flared. She felt claustrophobic in the small room, panicked about a possible fire, and wound up sleeping on the floor in her mother's room—a sequence that would repeat itself every night. Although Margaret was willing to switch rooms with Jackie, Jackie would not allow it. She was afraid her mother did not have long to live and wanted her to have the best room possible for whatever time she had left. There were no other vacant rooms with fire escapes available for Jackie, so the situation remained in this disturbing state.

Coupled with this, as the daily chore of preparing meals became a daily plight, Jackie and Margaret became angry at the lack of cooking facilities in the building. They said that the coalition had wasted their money on the building, because people still could not live decently there. The lack of cooking facilities forced the residents either to eat out of a can three times a day or to eat out, which is costly. Although Jackie and Margaret's combined room rentals cost less than most apartments in New York City, they still did not have quite enough money left over to eat three nutritious meals a day. This meant they were still partially dependent on the day and dinner programs for meal supplements, forcing them to bring the residue of homelessness with them to the SRO. Perhaps Karen was more comfortable with relying on the programs to assist her because she needed this help for more than simply a monetary reason. For Jackie, Margaret, and the others who had shopped and cooked for themselves all their lives, to be compelled to use the meal programs was demoralizing.

When I first heard these complaints about the SRO, something in me crumpled. After working with the program and shelter guests for almost a year, and putting so much hope into the SRO as a means of alleviating the desperate anguish of so many of the women, I did not want to hear these complaints. I did not want to look at the possibility that the SRO was not a reasonable solution to end homelessness. If this, and the few other nonprofit SROs that other groups were opening, was not a solution, what was there to hope for? The government was not responding appropriately to the crisis. What was the answer? Where should the hope lie?

After my initial disillusionment, after reflecting on the fact that the women I worked with had come from homes, real homes, with their own bathroom and kitchen, with more breathing space than the tiny rooms allowed, I realized they would never be satisfied at the SRO. And that lack of satisfaction was as it should be. Yes, it was better than the shelter, but it still was not good. For Margaret and Jackie, who had had a nice home before their years of homelessness, that this—these two small rooms—was what years of searching for an affordable apartment had yielded, was disappointing.

◆

Beth's transition was the most traumatic. After living at the shelter for approximately two years, she had become used to communal living, even if that communal living was in dismal conditions. The shelter had become an institution to her. Beth had developed a fear of sleeping alone. On her second night at the SRO, Beth called the shelter from a pay phone on a street corner, begging to be allowed back in. Maria, my old supervisor, allowed Beth in for the night and told us what happened the next day.

I spent a lot of time talking to Beth in her room to try to make her feel more comfortable in it. I felt I was watching Beth fall apart before my eyes. She had always been so alive, so bright, so mentally sharp. Now she spoke about how the man living across the hall from her was able to materialize in her room by slipping through the keyhole, how he was sharpening a meat-chopping machine outside her door all night, which he intended to use to make sandwiches out of her, and so on. Beth knew she was saying things that did not make sense, and I think this scared her, too. She frequently said things like, "Now I know you're going to think that what I'm saying sounds crazy, but it's really true."

It was a difficult situation. She was embarrassed by what she was saying, but at the same time she believed what she was saying was true, the dichotomy adding to her confusion. Beth's reality became a series of threatening sights and sounds. She did not come to the day program where the health team could have spoken to her, and she refused to speak to an elderly female psychiatrist who had volunteered to visit her in her room. Beth had not been back to the shelter since the second night, but then we found out she had been spending many nights sitting up in one of the local hospital emergency rooms where she knew several of the nurses.

Beth was often angry with me now, not wanting to speak more than a few sentences before rushing out the door. She spent very little time in her room. I am sure she felt betrayed by me because I had not really "done anything about the madman" across the hall from her, and yet she still had twinges of self-consciousness about her allegations. When I offered to sit up in a chair in her room all night to see for myself what was going on and to confront the "madman" if he showed up, she refused, saying he would not come if I was in the room. I think Beth was more afraid to confront the fact that she was losing some control over her faculties than anything else. It was heartbreaking to see this transformation. We hoped that as she became more adjusted to living in the SRO, the Beth we had known for so long would return.

So the scars of homelessness began to show themselves. Simply removing someone from a street or shelter environment could not erase the psychological trauma of the experience. I should have an ticipated that the wounds would heal so very slowly, but I had been too preoccupied with everyday crises to give it much forethought. Were they, in fact, wounds that *would* heal?

Chapter 9

Out to Lunch: New York City's Mental Health System

◆

$\mathbf{A}$ whole year had passed since I started the job. I felt as if several years had been packed into one. I felt very tired. Besides the constant level of stress inherent in working with issues of homelessness, I found less job satisfaction in my new role as program director, and I missed the relative autonomy I had in running the shelter. I now had an "office" in the SRO—actually a tiny room, barely larger than a closet, behind the staircase on the main floor. I divided my time between the SRO, helping Joan at the day program, and stopping in to check on the dinner program. The soup kitchens practically ran themselves with the volunteers.

My dissatisfaction with my job was primarily due to recurring conflicts between Tracy and me. It seemed that I often had to go to battle in order to have a say in anything. Even something as basic as getting petty cash to buy the day program groceries turned into a fight. I was routinely laying out close to a hundred dollars of my own cash to cover expenses. We needed to set up a reasonable system to deal with this, but Tracy was overworked with the enormous task of building renovations and had little time to deal with the smaller details. Nevertheless, it was logistically important to me. I think Tracy wanted to be supportive, but she simply did not have the time. But I needed some support, especially since former support systems were no longer there.

I had previously attended the monthly board meetings and presented a written report on the month's activities. I used to enjoy these meetings and relationships I had with various members. Tracy decided this was no longer necessary and informed me that I was not to discuss anything with board members: she related things to the board, I was to relate to her, and Joan to me—that was the hierarchy. I was not used to such regimentation, it was not my style, and I did not think it was productive. I feared that as this bureaucratic "structure" was imposed, the day-to-day reality and problems of the homeless people we were all trying to serve would become more obscured, removed, distanced. And when policy is made in a vacuum, it can be dangerously far from the reality it is supposed to address.

Right or wrong, it was my style to try to make friends with the people I worked with, especially in such a small organization where morale and a sense of mutual support is important. Some people prefer not to get personal with people they work with, and this is a perfectly legitimate choice. So it was with Tracy. Our relationship remained on a business level. I simply did not enjoy this atmosphere very much.

I felt emotionally exhausted. While I seemed to be able to turn off the real work to a large extent when I was home, I began having a hard time turning off this ancillary stress. I wanted to work with homeless people, but I began to think my personality was too different from Tracy's to be able to work together reasonably. We finally had a big argument, which turned into a healthy discussion and cleared the air. I hoped things would be better now. But I was skeptical and began to look for another job in a shelter or other homeless program. And I was about to take a break.

I had taken four days off at the beginning of the new year, but volunteers had still called me late night and early morning hours at home to discuss problems at the shelter, so it had not been the most relaxing "vacation." I still had twenty days coming to me (one of the nice benefits of low-paying social service jobs), and I was planning to take it all in July and travel as far away as I could. This would be a real vacation.

◆

With my trip only a week away, Flossie, who had been at the shelter for well over a year, began showing signs of a mental breakdown. She had lived in her own world of voices since I met her, but lately her world seemed to be infused with a tremendous amount of anxiety and anger. My biggest hope for her was that we could get her hospitalized. I usually had mixed emotions about psychiatric hospitals, but since no one at the shelter had been able to penetrate her world, I still hoped that intensive services within a hospital setting would enable her condition to be stabilized. We had made little progress in this respect since the day I had first spoken with her.

Flossie had come to my office during my first week of work, eagerly asking for help with finding an apartment. She had been searching for a place to live for many months without uncovering any prospects. When I questioned Flossie about her last permanent living situation, she explained that she had been living with a man. She became pregnant and he had thrown her out when the baby was born. Flossie said the baby was now in foster care, and she was visibly sad and confused about the experience.

Flossie was an overweight woman in her early thirties who still had an abundance of baby fat on her large frame. Her long, thick hair was parted on the side and wrapped rather loosely in a bun at the nape of her neck, accentuating the roundness of her face. Her facial features were nondistinct and framed by 1950s cat-style eyeglasses, behind which her small, brown eyes held a somehow adolescent look as she stretched her neck forward and asked for a home. Flossie had a curious way of wearing her clothing inside out, except for the oversized trenchcoat she wore over several layers of clothing, usually pants, then a skirt, and several blouses.

I had been startled by Flossie's ability to express herself so coherently and, in fact, charmingly, as I had seen her talking almost incessantly to herself during my first few evenings at the shelter. Talking to oneself is not unusual, but the act of carrying on an active conversation with oneself is a bit out of the norm. Flossie responded to herself, two rivers of words interacting, engaging, as if two personalities dwelled within her one mind. It was fascinating to witness these discussions, and I was surprised at her ability to communicate so well in my office, despite snippets of interjected dialogue. Flossie also had her characteristic fits of uncontrollable giggling during our discussion, but had explained her situation very clearly.

Insecure, shy, yearning for affection and approval, Flossie often exhibited these feelings in a childlike way, the nervous giggles trying to mask anxiety and fear. The vulnerable child in her once propelled Flossie to give me a gift of a yellow, plastic duck filled with shampoo; to fill in the names of the three old ladies whose beds were closest to hers under the "family" section of her food stamp application; to send Joan a greeting card on which she wrote "Happy Universe, Love Flossie and all the girls." But there were also behaviors, albeit less frequent, emanating from a very unchild-like source. Wandering the streets spewing vile language, screaming out bitter hatred towards the men that had left her, angrily smashing empty bottles on a street corner when she thought no one was looking, the dialogue continuing to flow.

Each month, Flossie got a $331 SSI check for mental disability, which went into her account at the shelter. We encouraged Flossie to spend some of her monthly checks on clothing, food, and other items she needed, but she refused to spend any of it, so that she would have a healthy amount saved with which to secure an apartment and associated necessities, like furniture and a telephone. Since available apartments always cost more than she could afford, Flossie thought that the more money she saved, the greater her chances of eventually being able to afford one. That seemed sensible enough; however, if an SSI recipient's bank account exceeded $1,500, the SSI checks were cut off until only $1,500 or less remained in the account. The rationale is that if a person can save so much money, they must not really need it, so the government should not continue to supply it. Nabbed again by catch-22, but Flossie could not understand the catch. The policy was so preposterous to her that she did not believe it and continued to save every penny from her checks. When her account reached $1,500, her checks stopped coming.

It was difficult to imagine that Flossie could handle an apartment on her own even if she could finance it. Flossie had never lived on her own and so never had the opportunity to learn how to manage her finances, provide clean clothes for herself, cook, shop, or take care of an apartment. Perhaps she could learn these things with time and training, but she was not going to learn most of these skills in the chaotic environment of the shelter. Flossie often asked if there was a "sanctuary" where she could go; she sought a haven from her misery, a place to feel safe.

Joan had discussed psychiatric residences with Flossie, places where she could live with a small community of people with similar mental difficulties in a home that provided supportive services. Flossie was receptive to the idea. Psychiatric residences require that applicants have a history of some form of past hospitalization. Although Flossie was very vague about her past experiences in hospitals, it was clear from what little she said that she *had* been hospitalized at some point. That much known, Joan began investigating residences, suspecting they would all be full but that she could put Flossie on waiting lists.

Joan went through the reference book of psychiatric residences, calling for referral procedures and additional information on the homes that seemed appropriate for Flossie. Catch-22 again. Besides the fact that the waiting lists were several years long, there was a special admitting form that had to be filled out in a psychiatric hospital in order to even have one's application considered by any residence. Without that form, there was no hope of even getting on a waiting list. Flossie would not voluntarily go to a hospital. Like many former psychiatric patients, whatever her previous experiences had been scared her enough that she had a strong resistance to the very mention of the word "hospital." So the form could not be filled out, and the residences remained beyond her reach.

As months claimed the dreary succession of shelter days, Flossie became so disoriented that it did not seem prudent to move her into the SRO when it opened. Her inner voices had become more distinct and more angry. Flossie disappeared in early June, having given no indication that she was leaving or that she had found any place to go. She returned several days later in a greater state of confusion and anger, recounting in almost inaudible mutterings how she had been staying in an apartment with a man she had met. Flossie had been there for a few days when he said he wanted to go for a drive with her. He took her to an area of the city that she found unfamiliar and frightening and he left her there. Flossie was petrified. She eventually found her way back to the shelter, still in shock that she had been abandoned again.

A week later, Joan happened upon Flossie on a street corner that was close to the day program. Joan asked her what she was doing, as Flossie was bent over a small, burning parcel. Flossie said she was cremating a dead mouse she had found in the gutter. A few days later, she tied a dead pigeon to the front door of the day program. These bizarre incidents concerned us greatly, as her anger and preoccupation with death seemed to be escalating. The health team, which visited her twice a week at the programs, was powerless; she was not suicidal or homicidal, and she refused to take medication. Medication is not an easy remedy—some people do not respond to medication and the psychotic thoughts remain uncontrolled. Many medications also have side effects, but at least they offer the chance of some relief. With no psychiatric residences open to Flossie and no way to hospitalize her, we could only keep trying to convince her to accept the health team's medical intervention. And we watched her psychological pain grow as we stood by in helpless frustration.

We noticed a change in the texture of the dialogues Flossie had with herself. Instead of the usual banterings and giggling back and forth, another personality seemed to emerge from time to time. Her general demeanor was childlike, apologetic, and timid; the new one was vicious, vengeful. The vengeful personality spoke with a different voice than the one Flossie normally used, speaking with something of a British accent and using vile language, which was uncommon from Flossie. Her posture also reflected the personality that she portrayed, hunched and cowering as the child, erect and imposing as the avenger. Most of the time she was her usual chattering self, but I witnessed two or three brief appearances of the avenger during the last week in June, a week before my vacation was to begin. The avenger spoke of violence. The final appearance was at the day program.

Flossie was lying on a couch at the program, presumably taking a nap. Joan and I were both at the program, as were two volunteers who were getting ready to leave. Joe, the church sexton, was walking across the program room to reach a storage area when Flossie bolted from the couch like steam from a geyser. The avenger was with us.

"I'll kill you! I'll kill you! Get away from me! I'll fucking kill you! I saw you. Don't come near me. I'll kill you."

The words poured forth in a seething torrent. The other women were shocked by the onslaught, as was the startled Joe, standing on the other side of the room. Joan walked calmly over to Flossie and said in a relaxed voice, "It's okay, Flossie. Take it easy . . . ."

"Get away from me!" Flossie screamed through clenched teeth, lurching forward menacingly.

I was a few steps behind Joan, and we were both surprised at the aggression Flossie had turned towards her. It was as if an invisible circle was drawn around Flossie, and anyone who stepped within its bounds was subject to attack.

"Flossie, calm down," I said steadily, "no one's trying to hurt you."

"I'll kill you, too," she spat, darting forward threateningly again.

She continued to scream along the same vein as I walked over to the telephone on the desk, deciding on the way whether to call the police. I did not think Flossie was dangerous as long as no one went near her. She was more scared herself than anything else. Yet there was an element of doubt, and with a few other mentally unstable women in the same room who might unwittingly provoke her, I was not going to take any chances. Coupled with these considerations was the thought that we could probably get her hospitalized in this state, and she would finally get some much needed help.

As I reached the desk, one could almost see an electrified current zip up Flossie's back as she looked at my movements and immediately sized up the situation. It was instantly apparent that she had been through this routine before and did not intend to take a trip to the hospital.

"I'm getting out of here!" she yelled. She charged towards the coatrack, grabbed her trench coat, and flew up the stairs and out the door. It all happened in a few seconds. We stood there gaping for a moment.

"Joan, I'm going after her," I said. "Who knows what she'll do. Make sure everyone's okay down here and then come follow me."

Flossie was already halfway down the block, screaming obscenities at the top of her lungs. When she glanced over her shoulder and saw me walking out of the church, she became more hysterical.

"She's after me," she shrieked. "She's going to kill me! Get her away from me."

Wondering what I had gotten myself into, I followed Flossie down the crowded avenue, packed with people out for lunch. Flossie continued screaming, half running as she forged her way through the crowds. Her body weight slowed her down, so I only had to walk briskly in order to keep a half block between us. I was not sure what I was going to do, but I knew I did not think it was fair to Flossie or the people around her simply to let her take off in the state she was in.

Flossie stopped running halfway down a block to catch her breath, turning to scream at me incoherently. I, too, stopped and stood quietly on the corner. A lumbering bus pulled up and opened its doors right in front of Flossie. I thought I was seeing things. A more ironic moment I had never experienced: Flossie had inadvertently halted at an unmarked bus stop. The second hung momentarily and then was gone. Flossie had looked at me, looked into the bus, looked at me, then bolted into the bus. The doors shut, and it pulled away from the curb just as Joan caught up with me.

"Do you believe that?" I asked in disbelief. "A year of trying to get her help, and there she goes in a bus heading towards downtown."

It was all so absurd. So I did something even more absurd. I ran after the bus, catching up with it as it slowed for a traffic light. I knocked on the door, which the bewildered bus driver, already nonplussed by the screaming Flossie, opened. I stood there. I stood there a second more, as I noticed the entire busload of people waiting to hear what on earth I was going to say.

"I'm a social worker. I've been working with this woman. She's been threatening people, and I suggest you ask her to step off the bus," I said, trying to be calm. Flossie dashed off the bus before the driver even gained control of his vocal cords. He closed the doors and pulled away. Flossie was on the run again.

"This is ridiculous," I said to Joan. "She's not stopping long enough for me to call the police and give them a location. What am I supposed to do, call 911 and tell them a woman is flying down Fifth Avenue?" Faced with absurdity, I did the absurd and called the police to tell them I was following a mentally disturbed woman who was running down the avenue, and I gave them a general physical description of Flossie. When I got off the telephone, I found Joan just two blocks away. Joan said Flossie was around the corner peeling off the outer layers of her clothes. She thought if Flossie did not see us, she might stay in one place. But we could not see around the corner, so I went into a bank on the opposite corner and watched Flossie through the cinnamon-tinted window panes as Joan stood down the block to flag down the police. Five minutes went by. And another five. I felt uncomfortable behaving like a spy in the bank. Another minute went by, and Flossie took off again.

Joan and I followed at a distance as we heard the police sirens. Flossie heard them too and reacted like a trapped animal before slaughter. She panicked as the police car and ambulance approached, and charged wildly across the intersection of oncoming cars. Two policemen jumped out of the car and ran after her, Joan and I on their heels. The police caught up with her and began talking to her when Joan and I came upon them. My heart sank. Flossie had reverted to her childlike self.

"Hi Lisa," she said meekly. "I'm sorry I caused you girls trouble," she half giggled. "Everything's okay, it's okay, don't worry." She twirled her fingers nervously through her hair, her neck and shoulders slouched forward meekly. Within the blink of an eye she had been completely transformed.

"What seems to be the problem?" one of the officers asked me.

"Can I talk to you alone for a minute?" I asked, as Flossie, several other officers and many curious onlookers waited for my response. We walked a few paces away from the crowd.

"Look, I know this is weird," I said, "but that woman was violent a minute ago. She's been in the shelter since I started there last year. She's been snapping into a violent state more and more. She needs help. Can't we please have her evaluated at the hospital?" I pleaded.

"Well, I see no evidence of this behavior myself," he said, "but I'll take your word for it. Okay, we'll take her to the hospital, but only on the condition that you go with us in the ambulance so you can explain this to the admitting doctor."

"Sure," I said. "Thanks." He could have gone strictly by the book and saved himself some trouble in the process, so I appreciated his efforts.

I felt like a jailer. I truly believed hospitalization was Flossie's only chance for life at this point, rather than exile from life in madness and impoverishment, but I could not deny that the means we had just gone through were demeaning. I felt like we had just been on a lion hunt. What madness was I part of that I chose to chase a woman through the streets of Manhattan in order to get her hospitalized, had to connive a policeman, had to ride in the back of the ambulance, the hunter and the hunted? Our psychiatric system at work. I swallowed the taste of medicinal rot rising in me and avoided meeting Flossie's defeated stare. It was not easy. The back of an ambulance is not large, and there was a policeman and an attendant with us as well.

We arrived at the local city hospital emergency room within ten minutes. The police gave a brief report to the admitting doctor, who happened to be the head of the psychiatric department, and then left. Flossie was taken into an examination room by one of the nurses while I waited nearby at the nurses' desk. After a few minutes, the psychiatrist came over to the desk in a cavalier manner and announced that he was not admitting Flossie. I was stunned.

"Why not?" I blurted out.

"She's chronic, she's chronic," he said languidly, wincing his chiseled features in disgust. "She's a chronic schizophrenic. I see her on the streets in my neighborhood all the time."

"Yeeesss," I said, trying to make sense of what he had just said. I could not. "I don't understand," I said. "You seem to think she's sick, you got the report that she's become increasingly violent, so why don't you want to treat her?"

"Well," he pondered, not coming up with a response. "Let me talk to her again. Why don't you come in the examination room with me?"

I followed him into the small room, empty but for Flossie, sitting in one of the two chairs. He stood, one leg planted on the free chair, careful not to put a crimp in his carefully pressed suit. The even, white teeth flashed. "Now Flossie," he began pompously. "I can't help you here unless you agree to take medication."

So that was the game. She had resisted taking medication in their private interview, and he did not want to take the responsibility of taking a resistant, thereby more difficult case. It was so much easier, after all, not to bother and simply not admit her. Flossie did not catch onto this part of the game. She seemed to think that if she went along with this plastic mold of a man he would let her go.

"Yeah, yeah, I'll take medication," she said, assuming the role of the good child. "I know it'll be good for me, yeah, so . . . ," trailing off into self-conscious giggles.

"Good," he said, gesturing for me to follow him out the door. I followed him, dazed by what had just taken place. There had been no semblance of an in-depth psychiatric assessment. What there had been was a snap judgment and a total lack of sensitivity. I found him incredibly repugnant.

We walked to the nurses' station again, and this time he told the nurse to admit Flossie. Her query as to whether any medical evaluations were in order was met with a quick no.

"Well, since she'll be in the hospital," I said, "can she get a gynecological exam? She's been complaining of vaginal infections for a long time, but it's been difficult to pin her down to keeping a doctor's appointment, and it's hard to find a doctor who will even agree to treat her." (Private doctors are not obliged to accept Medicaid, and Flossie would become too agitated to wait the usual long hours before being seen at a clinic.)

"She doesn't need a gynecological exam. She's schizophrenic!" he exclaimed, as if that label lay bare everything there was to know about Flossie. "They all have sexual fantasies. It's all in her mind."

These retorts smashed into my head against my sense of disbelief. I fought to control the anger that bubbled inside me, threatening to choke back my words. "I'm sure many people do have sexual fantasies," I said, "but I'm talking about physical problems. She's often found trying to look into her vagina in the mirror in the ladies room at the shelter while she rubs all sorts of creams there. She's always stuffing paper towels into her pants, and she scratches herself all the time. I really don't think it's in her mind."

"Believe me, I work with these people all the time," he said nonchalantly. "She doesn't need one." And with that he turned around and walked away, dismissing me.

What a commentary on the quality of "care" people like Flossie get. That this man could become the head of a very large city hospital's psychiatric unit said something about the quality of the system. Role models like him could poison countless young doctors struggling to find their niche and serve within the system. I turned to face the nurse, who was stupefied after witnessing this outrage.

"Come with me," she said in a hushed voice. We went into a corner room, and she shut the door behind us. "He's an ass," she said hotly. "Don't worry. I'll talk to a nurse on the floor in the psychiatric unit and make sure she talks to Flossie about getting an examination. We can go around him." I thanked her, said a few choice words about Dr. Freud, and headed back to the day program. It had been an eye-opener of a day.

———————————————◆———————————————

Within days, I set off on my vacation. Dennis had been working on a consulting project in Malaysia for two months, and I was going to meet him in Hong Kong. My four weeks took me into other worlds, strange and exciting. We visited several countries, each with its own brand of incomparable poverty. The dung hut in Kenya represented riches to a Maasai tribesman, the corrugated metal shack in Hong Kong served as welfare housing, the cramped apartment dwellings in Beijing were the general expectation. Relativity. I realized that while I might think a shelter bed would improve a Maasai's life, a Maasai would miss the comfort of knowing his goats were underneath his straw platform bedding. We each see the world through our own eyes.

Our plane broke down over the savannah plains in Kenya. As our pilot tried to fix the malfunctioning propeller, we mingled with the Maasai tribespeople whose grazing grounds we had landed on. The Maasai carried hand-hewn weapons, wore brick-red, toga-like garments, with large bones, brass coils, and beads adorning ears, nose, neck, arms, and legs reddened with ochre. We all watched the pilot's efforts, they speaking Swahili, we English. One Maasai man looked with curiosity at the binoculars I was holding. I gestured to him, offering him a look through the lenses. As he held the binoculars to his eyes, several other Maasai gathered around him. Our friend, Peter, informed me that Maasai do not have a conception of individual personal property, lamenting that I had probably just given away his expensive lenses. As the Maasai laughed with delight as they looked through the lenses in wonder, I realized how very different our eyes were.

Poverty in its most basic definition is hunger and lack of shelter. Beyond that, defining poverty becomes very difficult. But there is also a spiritual poverty spawned by hopelessness. The feeling of defeat can strip the sense of joy from an individual in whatever world he or she lives. But on the African plains I felt a keen sense of joy, a thrill of life. The Maasai's material possessions were extremely limited, their housing and meals primitive according to Western standards. But they were not poor. Their basic needs were being met and their spirit was evident. It was invigorating to be in their company. Back home in New York City, I was greeted with the faces of despair and hopelessness. Poverty in its most basic form did exist side by side with the plenty that epitomizes New York City, and spirits were extinguished, bit by bit, in the struggle to overcome hunger and find shelter from the brutal elements of nature and a society that closed its eyes. Why was our society so blind? Maybe people did not know, maybe they were not allowing themselves to see with their hearts.

◆

When I returned to work, Tracy greeted me warmly. I was hopeful that it was the beginning of a better relationship. I held off on my job search and also began a personal project I had thought of on my trip. I would write about the things I had witnessed in New York City while working with the women. Maybe it could help people to open their hearts and join in finding a solution to homelessness. I decided to try to write for one hour every morning before I went to work.

Joan filled me in on what had happened during my four weeks away, as she now prepared to take her vacation. Flossie had been improving in the hospital, and they were talking about discharging her soon. Joan had not been able to learn where they intended to discharge Flossie, so I called her hospital social worker to attempt to learn the details. Flossie had a student intern social worker, Joyce, from one of the local colleges. Joyce told me that Flossie had a file at the hospital several inches thick, having been in and out of their psychiatric unit for years. Flossie had also been on their obstetrics unit on numerous occasions; she had given birth to six children there, all of them now in foster care. Adding to this surprise was the fact that Flossie's mother had come to visit her.

She was described as a woman well into her seventies, suffering from mental illness and confined to a wheelchair. She lived in the neighborhood in a studio apartment and had a live-in helper. This revelation explained mysterious outings Flossie had made in the past, often returning to the shelter with childish trinkets like miniature bottles of bath bubbles or toilet water, toy earrings or gum machine rings, which she would say she had received from an "aunt who passed through town." The psychiatrist now working with Flossie, Dr. Yakovitch, felt long-term hospitalization at Manhattan State Hospital would fortify the improvement in her condition, but Flossie would not agree to go and could not be forced to do so. Dr. Yakovitch's current plan was to discharge her to the shelter if she would be accepted back.

I felt a profound sense of disappointment. For a whole year I had looked upon hospitalization as something of a solution to Flossie's problems. I did not expect miracles, but I did hope that once there she would get the help she needed to at least improve upon her current situation. Suddenly, I saw the revolving door as the only exit from the psychiatric unit—the revolving door I had heard about and witnessed for so long, where people go in, get a bandage, get churned out, the bandage falls off, they go back in, and so on. But not Flossie! Surely not the revolving door for someone as sick as Flossie! But there it was. And there was nowhere to turn now. The system was closed.

I would not accept it. I contacted Maria and apprised her of the situation. She agreed with me that discharging Flossie back to the very environment where she had become sicker was wholly inappropriate and an easy way for the hospital to shirk more responsible planning. Maria agreed not to accept Flossie back on that principle, that it was inappropriate and unjust.

I called Dr. Yakovitch and convinced him to let me meet with him and Flossie. When I got to the unit, I was met by a changed Flossie. Her dialogue had ended, the voices joining into one. The spasms of giggles still occurred occasionally, but even these were kept fairly well under control. So the medication had apparently worked for Flossie. Her forthcoming discharge to nowhere seemed all the more senseless. Yet, Dr. Yakovitch was willing to discharge Flossie to the same degrading situation and environment she had come from, an environment incapable of providing the supports necessary for her to maintain some degree of mental health. I was mystified by the doctor's readiness to send Flossie back to the shelter.

The three of us sat in a circle in a small room. I asked Flossie how she felt, if she understood what medication she was taking and why, if she experienced any side effects, if she understood why she had been hospitalized. She responded rationally to all my questions, and said she felt calmer now and did not hear the voices she used to hear. We talked about the fact that she would be discharged soon.

"Flossie, Dr. Yakovitch said he talked to you about going to Manhattan State," I said.

"Yeah, but I don't want to go. I want to go back to the shelter."

"You told me you feel better now, right?" I asked.

"Yeah, yeah," Flossie answered. "I feel less nervous."

"That's good," I said, searching for the right thing to say. "We talked about how you felt out of control before. I don't want to see you get like that again. The medication seems to help you."

"Yeah, but I want to go back to the shelter," she said.

"Going back to the shelter right now is not an option. It's not a good place for you if you want to keep feeling better. You were threatening to hurt people a few weeks ago, remember? I don't want to see you get to that point again," I said, feeling very uncomfortable with the conversation as I searched for a way to be diplomatic. Dr. Yakovitch sat wordlessly in his chair. "Besides, you know we couldn't find housing for you. Remember we tried to find a residence for you? We couldn't do it. You'd have a better chance of getting into one if you stayed in the hospital for awhile. Residences want people who are able to maintain some control. If you stay on the medication maybe you'll continue to feel better."

"You don't think I can find an apartment, huh?" Flossie asked.

"No, I don't. First of all, they're too expensive," I said. "And you have to learn how to live by yourself, and I can't help you do that when you're talking to different voices you hear. If you go to Manhattan State, they will probably keep you there for about three months, according to Dr. Yakovitch. During that time, your social worker there can try to find housing for you. Flossie, you deserve more than a shelter bed for the rest of your life. If you go there, at least you have a chance."

"It really would be better for you," Dr. Yakovitch chimed in.

"You really think I should go?" Flossie asked, like a confused child.

"I really do," I answered. "I would go with you when you're discharged from here to make sure you get there all right, and to meet your social worker. Sometimes it helps if a social worker knows that you have people who care about you and who will make sure he or she does the job. Ann, the health team nurse, goes there a lot and says it's a good hospital. She said she would also check up on you and make sure you're treated well. Why don't you give it a try?"

"Well, okay," Flossie responded. "I guess I'll go."

"That's good," Dr. Yakovitch said. "I can start on the paperwork and we can have you transferred soon."

Dr. Yakovitch left the room, and Flossie and I talked a little longer before I left. I spoke with Dr. Yakovitch on my way out, asking him to be sure to call us as soon as he had a transfer date set so I could arrange to go with Flossie. So it *was* possible to get off the treadmill! I stepped onto the street, convinced that all Flossie needed was extra care and attention, both to enable the system to work and to help Flossie accept what it had to offer.

I called before the long Labor Day weekend to check on her discharge. No discharge date had been set yet. Coming back to work Tuesday morning, I called to check again. Flossie had been discharged. I thought it was a mistake.

"What do you mean she was discharged?" I asked in disbelief.

"She was discharged over the weekend by Dr. Yakovitch," the nurse informed me.

"But why wasn't I called?" I asked. "He must have known on Friday. I promised Flossie I'd go to the hospital with her."

"She didn't go to any hospital," the nurse said in a bored tone.

"What do you mean? Where did she go?"

"She was discharged to her mother's house. Her mother said she'd take her in for two days, during which time she's to look for her own apartment," she said dryly.

"What!" I shouted. "Discharged to her mother's house—for two days! She's expected to find an apartment in two days? On SSI, in her condition? What happened to her discharge plan? What happened to her transfer to Manhattan State? This is insane."

"Look, you'll have to talk to her doctor," the nurse said calmly. "I only know she was discharged to her mother's. Maybe she changed her mind about Manhattan State and wouldn't sign the papers."

"But why wouldn't Dr. Yakovitch telephone me then?" I asked. "He knew I was working with her and was willing to come talk to her. I just don't understand. He may as well have thrown her out on the street."

I was dumbfounded. My anger overcame me. Dr. Yakovitch knew Flossie could not find an apartment. He had to have realized that she would be back on the street again. Did he think her life and dignity were worth less than that of others? And if so, what did that say about his life's work?

Dr. Yakovitch never took nor returned my phone calls. Flossie showed up at the shelter within a few days, dejected, confused, homeless. She was accepted back to the shelter. There was no point in denying her admittance when the trump card had already been played.

I wrote a scathing letter to Dr. Yakovitch. Once again, Tracy and I were at odds. She had intercepted the letter and warned me not to send it for two reasons, the first being that I was "too emotional." But I *was* emotional and felt this was appropriate. This was Flossie's *life* we were talking about. The second reason was that it was important to keep good relations with the local hospital. The absurdity of that logic seemed to be lost on her: it would be difficult for them to provide worse service than they already were. Even if Flossie's treatment had been an aberration, I felt morally obliged not to let it go by without protest. I was not in the job to be given the "good business" award. I did it out of love, and if that meant I was emotional at times, so be it. Maybe the system needed more emotion and fewer good relations to make it work in a humane way. Without telling Tracy, I mailed the letter to Yakovitch and sent a copy of it to the executive director of the hospital. No reply.

Chapter 10

You Call This a Home?

◆

Slowly, slowly the women who had moved into the coalition's SRO were adjusting, although Beth was still having a very difficult time. Her departures from reality, though less frequent, still occurred on a regular basis. Anxiety and suspicion ruled her days, her fears overwhelming her, swallowing her, and then spitting her out in a weakened, fragile form.

Perhaps seeing the changes in Beth fed into a fear of change that Gloria felt, this fear preventing her from leaving the shelter. Gloria had refused a room at the coalition's SRO, claiming that she wanted to wait for a room at the downtown SRO where there were shared cooking facilities. But when a room became available for her there she turned it down. Gloria had also declined an opportunity to share a house with another senior citizen on Long Island after an arrangement had been worked out with a Long Island agency that matches elderly people with extra living space with senior citizens who are looking for a place to live. Gloria had agreed to meet the Italian-born senior citizen who had been referred by the agency and to consider moving into her home. But on the morning of the appointment, Gloria had backed out, refusing to meet the woman or enter into any further discussion about it. The new shelter director, Sheila, was contemplating whether to continue to shelter Gloria, given her refusal to accept permanent housing options. The settlement house staff was adopting a stringent policy, making shelter stay dependent on a woman's willingness to find or accept ways to leave. Coupled with this policy was the increasing fear of the possible health hazard Gloria may have been creating.

Gloria had had a very bad cough for months. The health team had given her medication, but Gloria had refused to take it. Like many people of her generation, she had a fear of doctors and medication, preferring to self-medicate with home remedies of different foods and well-known, over-the-counter medications. Gloria had been prone to coughs, but never before had she had a cough that lingered for so many months. It lingered, and it grew in intensity. Whether at the shelter, dinner, or day programs, Gloria's steady, rumbling cough could be heard. The women were afraid of catching it; the staff was afraid of worse. There had been a growing incidence of tuberculosis (TB) reported throughout the shelter system, a disease that is rare throughout most of the population in the United States but is common among people who live in crowded, unsanitary conditions. TB is contagious. The health team had informed us that given the intensity and longevity of Gloria's cough, TB was a possibility. The team could do a simple blood test to determine if she had it. Gloria refused the test.

The TB test, called the tine test, is one most people have had at some point in their lives: a nurse pricks one's skin with a short, four-pronged needle that has a circumference no larger than that of a dime. Less painful than a single-needle injection, if the pin pricks change color or swell within a day or two, the possibility of TB is indicated. The health team, Joan and I, numerous volunteers, and the other women at the shelter could not convince Gloria to take the test.

It soon became a public issue at the day program. Everyone knew Gloria posed a possible threat to their health, and they also knew that it was a possibility that Gloria might be thrown out if she did not take the test and the cough persisted. The other women were worried about her, and a small, internal campaign began to try to convince Gloria to take the test. Despite the fact that Gloria's stubborn, argumentative personality often got on people's nerves, many of the women had grown to care for her good heart, which she tried so hard to conceal. A few of the women offered to take the test with her in order to demonstrate that it did not hurt and was not harmful. Gloria would not budge. Nothing, no one, was able to penetrate the wall.

We called in a worker from Adult Protective Services, the public agency that exists to help elderly people who are at risk. A worker came to evaluate the situation after being informed that Gloria was on the verge of being thrown out of the shelter and day program due to the potential health hazard she was creating. The worker, like the rest of us, could not convince Gloria to take the TB test and could not force her to do so. Since there was nothing else she could do, she left, wishing us good luck.

Gloria had spit up blood in a coughing fit that week. Blood was one of the signs the health team told us to look out for, as the presence of blood in cough sputum is a strong indicator of TB. I felt we simply could not take chances anymore, and decided to ban Gloria from the day program. Once that decision had been made, the shelter followed suit, telling Gloria she could return to the shelter only if she took the TB test and got appropriate medical care. They also added the stipulation that she must avail herself of housing opportunities.

I had known Gloria for fifteen months. I had not come to know her history, but I had come to know *her*. And I was instrumental in throwing her out on the street. I knew that, in essence, it had been Gloria's choice to choose the street over the TB test, but I had set the ultimatum. I had decided what the rules of the game were. I had thought carefully about the rules and thought they were "right." But it was as if Gloria was playing on a different game-board. She refused to play on mine; she refused to try to win. So she chose the street—a seventy-five-year-old, arthritic woman, spitting up blood. She chose to sleep on the street. I felt helplessness and I felt sorrow.

Gloria slept wrapped in a blanket on the stoop outside the shelter. It was late September and it was getting cold. I could not understand how she did it, how she survived. Gloria was not a typical "street person." She had never lived on the street before, she had never known endless days without access to a shower, she had never felt the hard pavement beneath her arthritic bones. And yet she chose it over the shelter. Maybe the choice was not as clear-cut as I imagined it to be. Maybe a bed and heat did not outweigh the agony of being housed with eighteen other women, some with mental disabilities, some with physical disabilities, all with emotional pain from their circumstances. Maybe the collective pain in that room was harder to bear than the cold pavement hitting brittle bone and tired flesh. I could not know.

The health team visited Gloria on the street, giving her the over-the-counter cough medicine that she agreed to take. During the day, Gloria found refuge from the street at a local church with a sympathetic custodial staff. They allowed her to sleep in unused parts of the basement hall and to cook in the basement kitchen. The church staff was angry we had thrown her out. "How could you do that to an old lady?" they asked. The decision had been hard to make and was harder to live with, even though I thought it was the right thing to do. If only the world had remained in the black-and-white colors of my childhood; now most of the world seemed painted gray.

It was hard to come to work every day and face these issues. It was harder because Joan was leaving her job. She and her husband were moving to Boston. I felt a keen sense of loss. Joan had been working directly with the women at the day program every weekday for over a year. I depended on her for a lot—for doing most of the work at the day program, but also for moral support. It had been nice to come to work knowing Joan would be there with her usual good temper and sensitivity. She was one of those people you occasionally come across whose heart seems to be bigger than most. I could not replace her, but I would have to find someone to do her job.

It was a time when I began to wonder what I was really doing and what this was all about. I wondered how long I could work in the midst of chronic chaos and pain. I wondered how I could escape the chaos even if I was not in this kind of work. After all, I lived in the world. Desperate people were not going to disappear, even if I chose not to see them. And then there was the question: could I ever close my eyes, now that I had stopped to really take a close look?

The return of Natasha fortified my feelings of frustration. One day in October, Natasha returned to the day program eight months pregnant. She was twenty years old, unwed, unprepared. I thought of the baby she was carrying and what type of life the child was likely to have. I thought of Natasha's life and I could make a reasonable guess.

Natasha had come to us for the first time over a year ago. She was enrolled in a college preparatory course, had a grandmother who provided encouragement and support, was bright, and was eager to stabilize her living situation. Given these variables, it seemed her prospects for getting on her feet were good despite the tragic events she had recently experienced.

Natasha had been raised by her mother, an alcoholic and drug addict. She had never known her father, and had grown up in public housing in Queens with her mother, sister, and brother. While things had not been easy for Natasha, she seemed to have managed fairly well until problems stemming from her mother's addictions became more severe.

High on drugs and alcohol, Natasha's mother had beaten Natasha's younger sister on the head with a pot, giving her a concussion for which she was hospitalized. Child Protective Services then placed this sister, who was fourteen years old, along with her eight-year-old brother, in the custody of Natasha's aunt. The aunt's boyfriend sexually abused the sister, at which point the brother ran back to his mother's house, where he was allowed to remain. The sister wound up in foster care. Natasha was too old to be placed in a foster home and had come to the shelter in desperation, remaining in school and trying to hold her life together. She was very concerned about her brother and brought him to the day program one afternoon so Joan could help her enroll him in school again and refer him to a center that would give him follow-up social services. Although Natasha still communicated with her mother, she did not want to go back to the environment in the apartment and hoped to be able to find a place where she could start her own life.

A month or two after Natasha had come to the shelter, I heard about a brand new group home for young adult women opening in Brooklyn. The home was designed for young, single, homeless women who had a desire to go to school or job training and could benefit from a supportive living environment. Such homes are rare, and it was fortunate timing for Natasha. We helped her apply and she moved into the residence within a month. At first, Natasha loved it. She came back to the day program shortly after she had moved to the home to thank us for referring her there, giving us big hugs and smiles. I had felt a surge of happiness at seeing this woman have a chance for a better life.

Then it began to turn. The residence director called me a few weeks later to report that Natasha had begun to behave strangely as soon as the house had been filled to capacity (twelve women), picking fights with the girls and creating minor disturbances that seemed aimed at drawing attention to herself. The director was surprised at the sudden change from her former model behavior and wondered if it was linked to the fact that she was not able to devote as much time and attention to Natasha as she had during the first few weeks when Natasha was one of the first residents. She wondered whether I had seen Natasha behave similarly at the shelter. I had not and was very surprised to hear of the problems. The disturbances at the residence began to intensify as the fights became more frequent and spiteful. Natasha had also been seeking more attention from men by putting personal ads in the newspaper. Taking out personal ads is nothing new in New York City, but the residence director was concerned about the age of a man Natasha was spending time with, since he was more than twice her age. The director had the uneasy feeling that something was boiling up. A few weeks later, the house of cards collapsed.

The director called to tell me that Natasha had been caught stealing household items from the residence that week, items such as kitchen glasses and cooking utensils. Again, this behavior seemed to be aimed at getting attention more than anything else. She conjectured that Natasha's final stunt might have been driven by the same motive. That morning everyone had left the house to go to school or training, as required, but Natasha had run back to get something she said she had forgotten. Within the hour, the director had been contacted by the fire department. The house had been set on fire, a fire determined to be set deliberately and originating in Natasha's room. Fortunately, smoke had been spotted by a neighbor and the fire department alerted before the fire had done too much damage to the home. Although there was no conclusive proof that Natasha had set the fire, the director strongly suspected that she had done it. Not wanting to press an investigation that would ultimately hurt Natasha if she was found to be guilty, she decided not to press for one but would not allow Natasha to come back to the home. As it turned out, Natasha never attempted to go back, but she did show up at the day program a few days later to pick up a bag she had previously left behind.

When she came back that day, I asked her what had happened. Natasha was vague, using a childish manner of speech that she frequently lapsed into. The open bag she carried with her revealed some of the kitchen supplies the director told me Natasha had stolen. I asked her why she had done this. I was so sad and confused about it all. Natasha shrugged, tilted her head to the side like a shy little girl, and said it was because she did not like all the other girls being in the home. She had liked it better when she first moved in and spent more time with the director.

Something she had said once at the shelter flashed back to my mind. We had been walking down the stairs to the laundry room and quite out of the blue, Natasha had said she wanted to get pregnant. I asked her why, and she had responded, "So I could have something to love." The simple response had jolted me. Was there no one else for her to love? Was there no other way for her to feel loved herself? Was her yearning to be mothered herself so strong that she sought a way to create a mother/child bond of her own? Was the presumed simplicity and innocence of mother love the only love she could imagine that would not be enmeshed with intense pain? I wanted to cry.

Natasha skirted my questions about the fire, telling me she was going to live with her boyfriend. And she was going to have a baby. This current boyfriend was in his twenties, and they would be moving in with his sister and her six children, who all lived in a small studio apartment. When I asked Natasha if her boyfriend had a job, she said, "Yes, he steals VCRs off the back of trucks."

I could not comprehend. We were playing on different fields. Our rules were not the same, nor were our players, our equipment, our prizes. Maybe this young black woman felt she could never share the prizes I knew were available to me, and so she did not try playing my game. Maybe she had been taught by her mother and grandparents, who had grown up before this country witnessed the civil rights movement, that they as blacks would never be allowed to play on the white people's field. It is easy for white women and men to claim equal opportunity to the field and its prizes, while we know nothing of the black experience, nothing about what it feels like to have a legacy of slavery barely a hundred years behind us, nothing of growing up with the white world mouthing equality but often not believing it, nor willing to accept it. We are a long way from being color-blind. Skin color continues to shade our minds no matter how loudly we deny it. We live in a racist society that does not work hard enough at restructuring its worldview to truly *believe* in equality.

And so Natasha stood before me once again in October, eight months pregnant, hungry, having received no prenatal care. And she accepted this. This was life in her world, and I looked at her from mine, and felt the gulf that separated us, fearing that unless we start to build bridges, that gulf will expand and swallow us all. We talked, we ate, and she went on her way. And I wondered how long it would take for the love that she already felt for this child to turn to abuse or addiction amidst the poverty she lived in.

◆

In the weeks Gloria had spent outside, strangely enough, her cough had become much less persistent. The health team determined that since Gloria had responded well to simple over-the-counter cough medicine and had not produced any more blood, she could not have TB. We let her back to the day program, but the shelter would not readmit her because of her unwillingness to accept housing options.

With Gloria still sleeping on the sidewalk, Sheila had decided she could not continue to store Gloria's personal belongings at the shelter indefinitely. Not that Gloria had many things relative to an average apartment-dweller, but she had a lot relative to the other shelter residents. Gloria had taken more than her share of space. What this boiled down to was that Gloria had four large suitcases. After Sheila had spoken with her, Gloria came to the day program on the verge of hysteria at the thought of losing the few possessions she had left in the world. I agreed to store the suitcases in my office at the SRO, and we brought them from the shelter to the SRO together. It was a Friday afternoon.

After we got to my office and piled the suitcases into a corner of the tiny room, Gloria crumpled into one of the two chairs.

"How can she do this to me?" Gloria asked in a shaky voice. "Why? Why? What for? Leeza, tell me, tell me," she pleaded.

Throughout the ordeal of the past several weeks, Gloria had remained her stubborn, feisty self, maintaining her proud face to the world. This was the first time she became so outwardly emotional with respect to her situation. Her resolve was crumbling, and I hoped I could use that window to convince her to come in off the street. At the same time, it was very sad to witness Gloria trying to come to terms with her circumstances.

"Gloria, you know why Sheila is doing this," I said. "The shelter is not supposed to be for permanent use. It's *temporary*. You can't keep turning down permanent rooms and expect to be able to stay at the shelter forever. That's not what the shelter is there for."

"But Leeza, I want an apartment. My own place. Like before. I can't live like this," she cried, gesturing to our drab surroundings. "It's inhuman. Why did the coalition buy this? For what? To die in a little room? No room to move. No kitchen. No light. How can I eat? How can I live?" She broke down into heavy, loud sobs that racked her whole body. Strong, tough, stubborn Gloria. She was broken, and it was horrible to see.

"Help me, help me. Leeza, what I'm going to do?" she gasped between sobs.

But I had been trying to help her! Did she think I was holding back? Did she think I had a solution to her dilemma tucked away in some secret place? I looked at her old body rocking with sobs, and I felt a touch of her agony and desperation, which only she could fully feel exploding within her. Help? I had six-by-nine-foot rooms to offer. For the lucky ones, eight-by-ten. That is what I had—that, and my own sorrow and disgust, my own shame for having nothing else. Good intentions would not keep Gloria warm or soften the cement under fragile bones. I had small, run-down rooms to offer, with no cooking facilities and shared bathrooms. That was my offer; one could take it or leave it. I begged Gloria to take it. It was not a good offer, but at least it was something. It was not what the American dream has taught us to expect is our right: good living, where everyone has an equal opportunity for space and a chance to maintain a standard level of decency. But the American Dream has been changing. We no longer demand that the dream be available to everyone; we no longer pretend that it is.

"Take it, Gloria!" I urged. Don't you see? There *is* nothing else. This *is* the hope. This room.

We went in circles for close to two hours. For the first time I got a glimpse into Gloria's past. One of nine children who had grown up in Italy, she had lived with a brother and sister during her adulthood in a modest apartment on the West Side. After they died, she could not keep up with the rent on her own because of her very low Social Security benefits. Gloria became homeless, hanging on to the belief that she would be able to find an affordable apartment. She still did not seem to comprehend that finding an affordable apartment on her Social Security was not going to happen.

I went home. I left her standing on the sidewalk in front of the SRO. It was cold. It was the beginning of the weekend, and I left her there. I did not know what else to do.

◆

When I came in on Monday, the SRO's superintendent informed me that she had brought a chair out to Gloria on Friday evening, which she sat in for several hours. The sight of the old woman sitting out in the cold propelled a woman in the apartment building next door to ask Gloria why she was sitting on the sidewalk. When Gloria told her that she was thrown out of the shelter, the neighbor, Debbie, offered to let Gloria sleep on her living room couch for the rest of the weekend. (And they say New Yorkers are cold!) Leaving Gloria asleep on her couch, Debbie came in to talk to me on Monday to find out what options were available for Gloria. When she learned that we were more than willing to rent Gloria one of the rooms in the SRO, she was quite surprised, relieved, and a little bit angry that Gloria had not told her that piece of information. She was concerned that Gloria was already settling in to her apartment, which she had offered only as an emergency measure, not as a permanent home for Gloria. Debbie had two small children and very little space in her apartment. The living room Gloria was sleeping in incorporated a kitchen area and a bathroom; the front door and two bedrooms were accessible only by walking through this room. When Debbie learned that the coalition was still reserving a room for Gloria, she asked me if I would talk to Gloria with her to help her understand that the couch had not been offered for an indefinite period of time, especially since she had an alternative in the shelter.

When I walked into Debbie's home, my presence seemed to give Gloria a physical blow. She looked affronted, surely guessing what was to come.

"What did you come here for?" Gloria asked angrily. "Why you want to spoil things?"

"Gloria, you know why I'm here. Debbie told me she let you stay here this weekend, which was very nice of her. But she needs some space and privacy for herself and the children. She didn't know that you could have a room right next door. You can't stay here, Gloria. Debbie helped you out for the weekend, but she can't let you stay here. It's not fair to her and her children," I said.

"What you say that for?" Gloria asked, offended. "I like it here. There's plenty of room. The kitchen's right here. Everything's right here. Why can't I stay?" she asked, looking forlornly at both of us.

"I work late lots of times. The front door opens right into the living room," Debbie explained. "The living room is the only room in the apartment other than my bedroom and the boys' room. We want to be free to use it. Look, I tried to help you. I didn't want you sitting outside all weekend, but they say you can have a room at the SRO. You can visit. I'd pay you to babysit for the boys if you'd like. But then you'd have your own room to go to, and we'd have our privacy. It would work out much better," she said.

Gloria grew very silent, slowly gathering her things into her bag. She was mad at me. Very mad. She viewed me as the destroyer of her newfound home and could not seem to grasp that Debbie's willingness to take her in for the weekend did not necessarily mean she would be willing to let her stay there indefinitely. Debbie felt badly about the whole situation and so did I. Yet I was struck by Gloria's willingness to move in with this virtual stranger. Her rapid adjustment to living in Debbie's apartment gave me hope that once we got over the hurdle of getting Gloria into a permanent living situation, she would adjust and be relatively content.

I could have tried to convince Debbie to house Gloria for a longer period of time instead of taking the role I had, but protracting the process of moving Gloria towards a permanent home did not seem prudent. Debbie clearly was not willing to take her in indefinitely, so a few more nights, a week, a month, would only mean Gloria would be on the street again, and with the temperature several degrees lower. But I was the villain in Gloria's eyes. She would not talk to me.

---◆---

This time was not without its brighter moments. One night that week, I loaded a borrowed van with furniture the SRO superintendent was donating to Jean and Lily. Their studio had been completed, and they had already moved in, living with the sparce amount of furniture that came with the room. The superintendent donated a kitchenette table and chairs, sofa bed, bed linens, towels, bath mat, and several other household items, many of them unused. Two volunteers who knew Jean and Lily from volunteering at the shelter, Bruce and Judy Zuckerman, helped me load the van. It was their tenth wedding anniversary, and they had decided to spend it doing volunteer work as an expression of their love. We all felt lighthearted: Jean and Lily finally had their own place; it was newly renovated, spacious and clean; we had nice things to bring to them; Jean's housekeeping jobs were going well. In short, it was a happy ending for them. They went through hell to get there, but at least there had been relatively good things at the end of their ordeal. If they had not been fortunate enough to get one of those three studios in the building, the story probably would have had a much different ending.

Jean came to the office the day after we made the delivery with a box of candy to show her appreciation for our efforts. This was a pleasant surprise. We were much more used to having the anger and frustration people feel towards the "system" directed at us, the social workers. We, after all, are part of the system. We often feel like tightrope walkers: advocating for clients within the welfare, housing, and health systems, while our social work colleagues in government positions are often the ones we are directly combatting. Even in private organizations, we hold the power, not the client—power to admit someone to a shelter, SRO, or food program. Even if we try hard not to abuse the power, it inexorably colors the relationship. This uncomfortable position does not win friends easily. So when Jean came in with heartfelt thanks, it gave a lift to a spirit becoming disheartened by days of seeing Gloria on the sidewalk.

◆

Another weekend passed. Monday brought a new surprise. Sue, a board member and volunteer, had moved Gloria into the SRO over the weekend. Gloria and Sue had become friends since Gloria came to the shelter two years earlier. Like the rest of us, Sue had been trying to convince Gloria to accept a room. She sought out Gloria on the street over the weekend, and this time successfully convinced her that a room in the SRO was her best bet. Because of painful bunions and infirmities due to old age, Gloria had difficulty walking up and down stairs, so we had held a vacant room on the second floor for her (the first floor held only office space and the superintendent's apartment). Unfortunately, the room was one of the smallest in the building and had only one window that looked out onto the cement wall of the building next door, about eighteen inches away. At least she was off the street, and for that I was greatly relieved.

When I went upstairs to greet Gloria, she was grumbling up a storm about how tiny and dark the room was. I was glad she was mad—better that she be angry than depressed and passive. Providing her with the opportunity for the room was a step in the right direction, but it was nothing to be overjoyed about, so her emotions seemed apt. I think we, as a society, could do better. So I was glad she took the room and also glad she retained her fighting spirit. It is when we passively accept injustice that we are really in big trouble. I do not know why Gloria finally decided to take the room. Maybe it just got too painful outside. Maybe she believed if she kept fighting when inside the SRO, she could believe this was not the end of the line for herself. Maybe she could still retain hope for retrieving the modest life-style she once had.

I wrote to Joan to tell her the news. She had worked so hard with Gloria, and I knew she would be happy to know she had finally moved out of the shelter. I also wrote her that I had found a new program assistant, Mara, who had just started.

Mara was about forty years old and had a good amount of counseling experience behind her. She was serious about her work and had a feminist outlook that drew her to working with women. I was already enjoying working with her, both because of her pleasant personality, and her keen insights and fresh perspectives on assisting the women. Yet, I suspected our professional relationship would be short-lived. I was contemplating leaving my job.

Chapter 11

Checking Out

◆

November was upon us. Almost a year and a half working with the program, and I began to wonder more and more whether it was worth so much energy. How far had we come, after all? Did I help anyone measurably enough to warrant the enormous input of time and effort? Yes, a number of the women were now living in SROs, but was that enough? Was that worth the effort? Couldn't there be more? And what about the other women who were still in the shelter waiting for rooms, or forever unable to care for themselves? What of all the women, men and children in other shelters and on the streets? There were always more. More people begging for a sandwich. More people begging for a bed, for a room, for a job. More people begging.

The numbers were swelling, not shrinking. The city opened more shelters, churches opened their doors wider. What would stem the tide? The system was not working. It was out of control, and trying to work within it began to feel like a fool's errand. There was not enough housing; there were not enough mental health services; there was not enough food; there was not enough staff, security, medical services—there was not enough of anything! Whatever I had contributed towards a solution seemed very, very meager compared with the breadth of the problem. I was frustrated at the sluggishness of the system and society to move towards better conditions.

I had not made much progress on my book idea either. I just could not discipline myself to write on a daily basis in addition to doing my job. I believed that *maybe* if more people knew what homeless people had to endure and understood the complexities of the problem, we would, as a society, move more quickly towards change and solutions. I felt like I wanted to stand on a corner and shout about all the problems I had seen so that people would understand what was going on. If I left my job I would have more time to write, and maybe a book on the subject could help alter misperceptions and contribute towards positive change more than plodding along and trying to help one woman at a time.

One and a half years, and we had just scratched the surface of what Deirdre was about. Mara had been able to converse with her more than anyone had before at the program, and for the first time we got some clues as to what was on Deirdre's mind. One of the few things that Deirdre had made explicit from the start was that she was a vegetarian and also refused to wear anything made from animal hides, such as leather shoes. I thought she was just an animal lover. But after she spoke with Mara for five minutes (a record), we realized it was not that she was an animal lover. She would not eat or wear anything that had once been alive because she saw no difference between human beings and animals, and she thought it inhumane to hunt her own species. She had been hunted last summer in the park and knew what being prey felt like; she would not be party to a hunt.

Deirdre saw no difference between human beings and animals. Abject despair, hopelessness, emptiness. I could no longer turn off that part of myself that absorbed the pain and despair that I witnessed daily. The positive gains I had seen, the visible improvements in individual lives paled against the ever-present shadows of despair that loomed over me, finally engulfing me with their collective, insidious force. I began to lose perspective as the blackness drew me in, absorbing my energy and spirit. The collective pain of the past eighteen months seemed to hit me in a giant wave.

Flossie's revolving door. The degrading escapade we underwent to get her through that door. Complaints about the SRO. The women's emotional scars that would not heal. Leaving Hannah in the snow. Shelter was an emergency stopgap at best and was not even adequately meeting *that* need. The slowness of some of the women to change, like getting Louise to bathe. And then, despite the tremendous need, our inability to provide enough supports to help maintain that change. The women turned away with nowhere to go. The sense of failure at throwing out people like Norma, who were helpless to help themselves but who could not be helped involuntarily. Suzanne eating grass to stay alive. Gloria sleeping on the pavement. Natasha and her baby—what hope for them? Tiny bits of solutions here and there, never enough, never whole. I came back full circle to where I started out: "How can I help?" All this work, and I still could not really answer that question because the opposing forces within the system and society were so powerful, so pervasive.

My feelings of futility were compounded by other concerns. Tracy and I were getting along much better and had a decent working relationship, but we would never be on the same wavelength and the internal job stress was still higher than I would have liked. I also felt that the way my job had evolved diminished my ability to make a significant difference, even within the organization. I began to consider more seriously an option I had been toying with for a few months: leaving my job, modeling on a more regular basis to make ends meet and writing the book with the free time that gave me. I decided to do it.

I gave a little more than a month's notice, agreeing to work until after Christmas. I looked forward to the new year with great anticipation. I would be free.

◆

I met with Mara on my last day at work for one final supervision session. A few days earlier, she had spent Christmas day with the women at a church that hosted a turkey dinner with all the trimmings prepared by a contingent of volunteers. Mara told me how, at the group's request, Beth sang after the meal, performing the "Our Father" hymn in her lilting soprano voice. Mara was sitting in rapt attention, hands folded on her lap, when she heard an enamel-like, clacking sound against her bracelet. She picked up the object on her lap, supposing it to be one of her earrings. When Mara held the object closer, she realized it was a glass eye. One of the women, Cindy, had an artificial eye she had popped out. Mara said she turned around and handed Cindy the eye, whispering, "You dropped this." The performance continued undisturbed.

I had to laugh as I conjured up this scenario, so absurd as to be humorous. One complaint I could not make was that the job had ever been dull!

Tracy took me to a farewell lunch at a nice restaurant. It was the first time we ever had lunch together, the first time I ever learned anything about her personal life. I guess she just felt there were lines to be drawn which she chose to draw and I did not. Her heart was definitely in the right place, and she could not have worked harder or more hours to build the organization, but we just seemed to communicate in different ways.

After lunch, I went back to the day program to say goodbye to the women. Mara had organized a little farewell, with a cake set at the lunch table. We all sat around the table and Mara made a speech of sorts, with kind sentiments. She asked if anyone else wanted to say anything. The women were extremely quiet and reserved. No one said a word. Everyone stared. I got the sense that they felt like I was abandoning them, turning my back, running out. There were no hugs or kisses, no emotional goodbyes. Everyone remained in their seats. It felt unnatural, emotionally barren. Didn't anyone care that I was leaving? I had so many mixed emotions myself. I would miss the women, miss my job. The women did not understand or know all my reasons for leaving. What they did know for certain was that I was checking out and that they would remain. I felt a sense of guilt at the betrayal I sensed they felt. The silence blew through me.

I felt emotionally depleted as I walked out of the day program for the last time, heading straight for the airport to catch a plane to Seattle, where I would be spending the new year with Dennis's family. We had gotten engaged the week before. I had much to look forward to. I felt lighter, freer, as if the past eighteen months had slowly been cutting off my oxygen and now I could breathe again. The plane took off, and I had the marvelous sensation that I was leaving all those tiresome, complex, weighty problems of homelessness far behind me.

Chapter 12

Taking Stock

◆

One year later I went back to social work, working for Catholic Charities Office for the Homeless and Hungry. I viewed the homeless situation during the interim as an outsider, putting my thoughts on paper. I found myself drawn back to social work and homelessness, despite my frustration and disgust at the often seemingly impenetrable system. I realized I had allowed frustration at the system to turn itself into frustration towards homeless people themselves, and so I had turned away. The system is a complex, amorphous collection of ideas, institutions, laws, and economic forces that sometimes can appear to be beyond our control; it is easier to blame the system's victims, the scapegoats, the easy targets. But after stepping away, my mind's eye gradually cleared, helped along by recurring images of Beth, Gloria, Stacie, Jackie . . . .

I had stepped away, but I still had to step over homeless people on the street. They still prodded my conscience. And I realized they always would. You cannot feign blindness when your eyes have been etched with indelible images. I could not simply watch life from the outside as if it were a spectator sport. Life *is* the best teacher, and I realized I had learned numerous invaluable lessons about life from the homeless women I had come to know. I realized only when I stepped away how much they had enriched my life and the lessons they had taught me: strength, courage, humility, humor, generosity, love. I had had experiences I would not trade for any amount of money.

Dennis and I took our vacation the following year in India. We visited Mother Teresa's home for the dying in Calcutta and had the great fortune of meeting her. Systems, governments would change, but simple truths would live on. Start by picking up one person—if there is a need, do what you can to fill it. There was a tremendous sense of peace radiating from Mother Teresa and throughout the home despite the difficult circumstances. Who knows why?

I am still frustrated by the feeling that a single individual may not effect great change. But as Mother Teresa's example exhibits, whatever positive contributions each person makes moves us further along towards a just, compassionate society—a society nurtured by hope, rather than despair. Every drop does count, does add to the pool. And in the process, lives are affected, some situations improved.

I have no grand solutions to the homelessness problem. There is no magical answer. There are a number of suggestions and approaches that many have made, a few of which I echo: more low-cost housing, more supportive housing for those who need help, more community-based psychiatric services, more drug programs, job programs, more recognition of self-help efforts by homeless people who must be part of the dialogue about solutions, and more coordination of all efforts. But few of these can be implemented without society's empathy, support, and acceptance. We need to create the will to implement solutions. What we must start with is compassion. We need a society that values human life at all costs.

We often see the opposite. Neighborhoods band together to keep out low-income dwellings; people learn to deflect their eyes from the homeless man lying on the sidewalk; neighbors protest against the soup kitchen line that forms on their block. To love those "different" from us—poorer than us, darker than us, sicker than us, hungrier than us—means we must be open to self-reflection and self-sacrifice. It means we have to stop and care, reach out, compromise, change. We must look for the similarities instead of being fearful of the "differences." Or perhaps we also fear those similarities, for if we can see ourselves in a homeless person, might not that be us but for a chance circumstance? "Who is my neighbor?" the parable of the good Samaritan queries. Everyone. We are all neighbors. We must act on this rather than become a society of isolated, fearful strangers.

Many people give their time for those who suffer as they volunteer at shelters and soup kitchens, become politically involved in issues that affect the underclass, welcome programs that will help homeless and hungry people in their neighborhoods, encourage and support homeless people who are engaged in creating change. They stop to care, giving off light, kindling hope. For those who exist in crowded, unsafe city shelters and welfare hotels, the light is not yet bright enough. It cannot illuminate the darkness of their days.

We can eradicate homelessness and hunger. But only if we create a collective will. We might have to get up early so we can buy coffee for the man we pass on our way to work, or pay higher taxes so we can build low-income housing, have a residence for the mentally ill built in our neighborhood, admit our educational system is failing and do something about it, have low-income residences on our block. We might have to suffer the discomfort of serious self-reflection to purge ourselves of prejudice and fear. We might have to shatter our complacency by opening our eyes to the pain of others. We might have to share in some form of suffering so others might suffer less. We can refuse to accept homelessness. But are we willing?

Dennis and I moved out of New York City two years ago. I stay home to raise a wonderful little baby daughter. I hope by the time she can speak we will not have to explain to her why people lie on the streets and at our feet. I hope homeless people have not become a permanent part of our society.

For awhile I kept abreast of how many of the women were doing. At last check, Margaret had eventually decided to have her tumor operated on and had completely recovered. Jackie graduated from a pet-grooming school. Both moved in with Elsie, whose health had deteriorated so greatly that she could no longer live alone, and the three women decided that the shared, crowded apartment was the best arrangement they could find. Beth never regained total control of her mental faculties and declined to such a point that she had to be placed in a nursing home. Stacie was managing in the uptown SRO quite well until she developed cancer, which eventually took her life. Jean was still working for the original couple that hired her; Lily, increasingly frail, remained at Jean's side. Gloria was still complaining about her room, still relishing a good cup of espresso and old Caruso records.

Suzanne was picked up by a downtown outreach team that was eventually able to hospitalize her. I spoke with her at the hospital right before she was to move into an adult home in Brooklyn. Another outreach team responded to complaints about Hannah, who was living on the street and lighting rubbish fires to keep warm. The last I heard, the team was fighting through the court system to get her hospitalized in a long-term facility. Kathy moved out of state to live with her boyfriend on his aunt's farm. Months after Michelle was thrown out of the shelter for failing to look for work or apply for welfare, she ran into a volunteer and told her she was working again. Norma wound up in a supportive residence for ex-offenders run by a religious order. Louise was thrown out of the shelter for failure to bathe and was never seen again. Deirdre was thrown out of the shelter for failing to take any steps towards independence. Flossie and Emma were still at the shelter.

These are some of the lives that etched their pain and their spirit in my mind, becoming a part of me, enriching me, scarring me, as they were scarred with the agony of living in places that are a far cry from home.

About the Author

Lisa Ferrill is a social worker who has worked with homeless people, the elderly, and juvenile offenders. She received a bachelor of arts degree in psychology from the University of Notre Dame and a master's degree in social work from SUNY, Stony Brook. Lisa is currently living in Boston with her husband and daughter.